Tarot
& Other
Divination Arts

D1190502

Tarot

& Other

Divination Arts

Learn to foretell the future

Alice Ekrek & Michael Johnstone

This edition published in 2021 by Arcturus Publishing Limited
26/27 Bickels Yard, 151–153 Bermondsey Street,
London SE1 3HA

Copyright © Arcturus Holdings Limited

All rights reserved. No part of this publication may be reproduced,
stored in a retrieval system, or transmitted, in any form or by any means,
electronic, mechanical, photocopying, recording or otherwise, without
prior written permission in accordance with the provisions of the
Copyright Act 1956 (as amended). Any person or persons who do any
unauthorised act in relation to this publication may be liable to criminal
prosecution and civil claims for damages.

AD008818UK

Printed in the UK

CONTENTS

INTRODUCTION

Most of us attempt to foretell the future on a daily basis, although we may not think of it like that. From the banker who tries to predict which stocks will rise and fall to the grocer who tries to foresee how much a customer will buy of a particular product, we are all amateur soothsayers at some point in our lives. However, we also wish we could predict the future in less prosaic areas of life. What personality will our unborn child have? When will we meet our great love? Should we take that new job out of town? If only we had a crystal ball to peer into and discover the answers… well, we do!

You can use the techniques in this book to discover what will happen in your life through traditional methods of divination such as the tarot, palmistry or even gazing into that crystal ball we just mentioned.

The history of fortune-telling is a long and illustrious one, but this is not a history book. It is a practical guide comprising the work of experts in the field of divinatory writing. Tarot reader and author Alice Ekrek introduces us to the tarot and how to read it. Her enlightening guide to this fascinating subject will enable you to begin your journey into the life lessons the cards can provide. If you don't own a tarot deck, we also show you how to use an ordinary pack of cards for the same purpose.

Everyday ease with divination is continued in Michael Johnstone's sections on tea leaf reading, crystal divination, numerology and palmistry. The gifted astrologer Marion Williamson answers that question about a child's personality with her guide to astrological knowledge. In short, if you are in need of some guidance through more mystical means, our writers can enlighten you with this introductory guide to some of the more famous divination methods.

What is divination?

Divination is:

1. The action or practice of divining; the foretelling of future events or discovery of what is hidden or obscure by supernatural or magical means. Also, with a [article] and pl. [plural] an exercise of this, a prophecy, an augury.

2. Successful conjecture or guessing.

Not content with telling us that the word 'divination' is a Middle English one that has its roots in Old French or Latin, and then defining the word, the 1983 edition of the Oxford English Dictionary goes on to tell us that the first recorded written use of the word in its longer meaning is found in the work of Sir Thomas North (c. 1535–c. 1601). The Tudor poet wrote, 'The flying of birds, which doe geue a happy divination of things to come.' The second meaning was first used in written form by North's contemporary, William Shakespeare, who in Henry IV Part II wrote:

'Why, he is dead.
See what a ready tongue suspicion hath!
He that but fears the thing he would not know
Hath by instinct knowledge from others' eyes
That what he fear'd is chanced. Yet speak, Morton; Tell
    thou an earl his divination lies,
And I will take it as a sweet disgrace
And make thee rich for doing me such wrong.'

What the dictionary definitions fail to do is give any hint of the breadth of the ways in which the action of divining can be practised. For that we must move several centuries on from Thomas North and William Shakespeare and turn to twentieth century technology – the internet.

Switch on a computer, select a search engine and key in the word. Google alone offers over 16,700,000 sites to choose from! Hitting on one or the other of them will eventually lead to an extraordinary assessment of methods by which the future may be foretold. What follows was compiled by an organization called BoxArt and is reproduced here with its generous permission.

Aeromancy

This form of divination looks to the air and sky for inspiration, particularly concerning itself with cloud shapes, comets and other phenomenon not normally visible in the heavens (see also Meteoromancy).

Alchemy

The much sought after but never achieved practice of transmutation of base metals into precious metals (e.g. gold or silver) with the aid of an esoteric third substance is a form of divination, seeking as it does to use 'divine' knowledge to alter things.

Alectryomancy

Those who divine by alectryomancy encourage a bird to pick grains of corn from a circle of letters. The letter closest to the grain pecked is noted and the words eventually formed used as an augury. A variation is to intone the letters of the alphabet at sunrise, noting those at which the cock crows.

Aleuromancy

Anyone who has ever eaten a fortune cookie has knowingly or unknowingly indulged in aleuromancy whereby answers to questions are rolled into balls of dough, which once baked are chosen at random by those who have questions to ask.

Alomancy
Also known as halomancy, this form of divination involves studying the patterns made by table salt poured from the hand of the practitioner onto a consecrated surface or small area of land preferably used only for the purpose of divination.

Alphitomancy
Baking is the media by which some diviners look to find the truth. Specially baked cakes are fed to those who stand accused of a misdeed of some sort, to establish guilt or innocence. The cakes are digestible by someone with a clear conscience but are unpleasant to those with guilt written on their minds.

Anthropomancy
Now long-outlawed, anthropomancy is a means of divination that involves human sacrifice.

Apantomancy
The chance meeting with animals such as black cats, many types of birds and other creatures is believed by some to be a sign of things to come. The siting of Mexico City was a result of apantomancy. According to legend, Aztec practitioners of the art saw an eagle, a live snake in its mouth, soar into the air from the cactus on which it had been perched, and took this as a sign that such a spot would be the place around which to build a settlement!

Astraglomancy
Sometimes known as astragyromancy, this method of selecting a path through the future uses special dice that bear numbers and letters on their sides.

Astrology
Those who practise this, one of the oldest, most popular and scientific forms of divination, look to the Sun, the Moon, the planets and the stars, and their position and passage through the sky to tell on whom the

Sun will be shining in future. The Babylonians practised the art, and it is more or less accepted by most people who have looked at the relevant research with an open mind that the Great Pyramid and other mausoleums in the Nile Valley were built with astrology very much in mind.

Austromancy
The way the wind is blowing is believed by some to provide a guide as to what prevailing currents hold in store in days to come.

Axiomancy
When an axe or hatchet is driven into a post, the way in which it quivers before settling is thought to provide a signpost to what will occur in the days to follow.

Belomancy
Similar to axiomancy (see above) the ancient art of belomancy looks to the flight of arrows and how they move when they hit their target to point the way to what lies ahead.

Bibliomancy
Diviners who practise this particular skill use books to thumb their way through the library of the future. A question is asked, the chosen book is opened at random, and the words on which the eye first falls are then interpreted to answer the enquirer.

Botanomancy
Botanomancers look to the shapes made in wood and leaf fires to discern future events.

Capnomancy
One stage on from botanomancy, capnomancy concerns itself with interpreting the forms taken on by smoke swirling upwards from a fire to help them peer through the veil that shrouds the future from the eyes of non-believers.

Cartomancy

Competing with astrology for the Number One spot in the top twenty of divination (in the West at least), cartomancy in any of its several forms uses cards to answer the questions that those who wish to look into the future ask. The cards may by those in an ordinary playing pack, or a specially designed one such as the Tarot.

Catoptomancy

This early form of crystal gazing catches moonbeams in a mirror turned towards the Moon and interprets the shapes and patterns they create to form a picture of future events and to answer questions as to which is the best path to tread through them.

Causiomancy

When an object is placed in a fire, it may burn, melt, change colour, evaporate and move or behave in a variety of ways. Causiomancers gaze into the flames at objects cast into them and draw their conclusions from the way they react to the melting heat.

Cephalomancy

The root of the word, the Latin 'cephalicus', itself derived from the Greek word for 'head' (kefáli), provides the inspiration for this particular type of divination, but gives no clue as to which particular type of head. In fact, those who divine via cephalomancy use the heated skull or head of a donkey or goat as the key that unlocks the door to future events.

Ceraunomancy

Many ancient peoples believed that thunder and lightning were one of the ways in which the gods communicated with each other. And as the gods were omnipotent, what better way to divine the future than to eavesdrop on their conversations, using thunderclaps and lightning flashes to give ceraunomancers the gift of foresight?

Ceromancy

Also known as ceroscopy, ceromancy practitioners pour molten wax into water and use the shapes taken on by the hardening substance as the clues that will unravel the mysteries of the future.

Chiromancy

Closely allied to palmistry, chiromancy concerns itself only with the lines of the hands to discern what tomorrow has in its grip, whereas the former uses other features of the hand to find out what lies in store.

Chirognomy

Like palmistry, this is another way of divining the future by observing the hand. Chirognomancers study its general formation rather than the more particular aspects considered by chiromancers and palmists.

Clairaudience

The word means 'clear hearing'. This method of divination is usually regarded as a form of extrasensory perception (ESP) whereby the unseen spirits who inhabit the future 'speak' to the select band who have 'the gift'.

Clairvoyance

Using their gift, which is another form of ESP, clairvoyants 'see' into the future, either during a self-induced trance during which pictures of future events come to mind, or in flashes that can come, unsettlingly, out of the blue. According to one claim, a passenger about to embark on the RMS Titanic had one such sudden clairvoyant experience as she was about to board the doomed liner and refused to sail.

Cleromancy

The shifting patterns of sea shells and pebbles on the beach, either moved by the flowing tide or taken from an appropriate beach and dropped from the hands of the diviner, are believed by cleromancers to help them dip into the waters of tomorrow. Another method of cleromancy is to hold a seashell up to the ear and listen. Most of us, when children, did this and were convinced we could hear the sea. Cleromancers with an ear for this sort of thing, believe that the gentle rushing that can sometimes be heard is a voice from the future telling of events yet to happen or trends that will gradually unfold as the tide of life ebbs and flows.

Clidomancy

Also known as cleidomancy, clidomancy uses the twistings and twirlings of a key suspended from a specially blessed or charmed cord to open the portal that shields the forthcoming (see also Radiesthesia).

Coscinomancy

Whereas clidomancers use a key, coscinomancers use a suspended sieve to solve the riddle of what is around the corners we must turn as we move through our lives (see also Radiesthesia).

Critomancy

This comparatively (very!) obscure method of peeking into the future involves baking special barley cakes. The way they take shape in the oven and the patterns the crumbs make when the cakes are being eaten, are the things that those who bake them hold to be significant.

Cromniomancy

Not much is known about this old method of divination other than that onion sprouts were thought to be able to provide pointers to the future.

Crystallomancy

When we think of divination or, to give it its more common name, fortune-telling, one of the images that comes to mind is probably that of an old woman peering into her crystal ball and via it into things to come. Fortune-tellers are crystallomancers by another name. It need not be a crystal ball: any crystal on which the seer is properly focused can be used. Some crystals are said to have special powers and are used for their own purpose. Sunstone, for example, is reputed to be an excellent conduit for those seeking knowledge of future matters of a sexual nature, while rose quartz has the reputation for helping those seeking advice on love.

Cyclomancy

The behaviour of a turning wheel, how long it goes round for and the directions or things to which its spokes are pointing when it comes or is brought to a halt, are all scrutinized by cyclomancers in their search for answers as to what's going to happen during future spins of the wheel of life.

Dactylomancy

This is a branch of Radiesthesia (see below) that uses a ring suspended on a piece of string or specially consecrated cord to peer into the mists of time to come.

Daphnomancy

People who divine using daphnomancy as their chosen method do so by burning laurel branches on an open fire and interpreting the resulting crackling that fills the air. Laurel is a wood that was sacred to the Ancient Greeks, who believed that it communicated the spirit of prophecy.

Dendromancy

Like daphnomancy (see above) wood is the key to this method of divination, in this case either oak or mistletoe. The former was sacred to the God of Thunder because it was thought to be the most likely tree in the forest to be struck by lightning and was therefore a conduit to him, and thence to others in the pantheon. Mistletoe was held in great veneration by the Druids and, later, was thought to be the wood from which Christ's cross was made.

Dowsing

This is the method by which the presence of water or precious metals is divined by using a forked rod that vibrates when held over the spot where what is being searched for is to be found. Hazel is the favoured wood for the purpose. Many people scoff at the very idea of dowsing, but there are too many records of times when it has been used successfully to detect water when all other methods have failed, for it to be derided by non-believers.

Geloscopy
This curious way of divination uses the tone of laughter as the way to find out what is about to happen to whoever is amused.

Genethialogy
This is the branch of astrology that predicts the path a person's life will take by plotting the positions of the stars and planets in the various astrological houses at the time of birth. It is one of the few methods of divination that lends itself to twenty-first-century technology! Anyone who wants to use genethialogy to find out their destiny needs only access a suitable website, and key in where and exactly when they were born. Once credit card details have been cleared, a detailed analysis will come on screen, which is simply downloaded to be constantly at hand.

Graphology
Handwriting has long been held to provide a key to character analysis. Indeed, some firms have such a strong belief in graphology, that they will not offer employment to anyone whose handwriting does not come up to scratch. Of course, if you know what characteristics are desired, with a little work you could ensure your success.

Gyromancy
This is a particularly active form of divination whereby the diviner walks around a circle, marked with letters at various points around its circumference, until dizziness sets in. This causes the diviner to stumble at different points, the letters at these points eventually spelling out a prophecy.

Haruspication

Perhaps one of the most famous of the ancient methods of divination, haruspication involves inspecting the entrails of an animal. It was widely practised by priests in ancient Rome: Shakespearean scholars will recall that in The Tragedy of Julius Caesar, the eponymous hero's wife, Calpurnia, warns him not to go to the Senate on the fateful Ides of March because of what has been foretold by priests who used this art.

Hieromancy

Also known as hierscopy, hieromancy is divination by observing objects of sacrifice – how they move in their death throes, how the blood flows and the shape the eventually lifeless form takes. It is now illegal in most parts of the world, but is probably still performed in regions where animism is the prevailing religion.

Hippomancy

Hippomancers divine the future by watching horses, taking note especially of their stomping and neighing. The art was probably developed among tribes of Native Americans and was observed by settlers on the trek west as still being practised by native tribes well into the nineteenth century.

Horoscopy

This is more or less another name for astrology, involving the use of astrological horoscopes to divine the future.

Hydromancy

Watching the water – its colour, ebb and flow, and the ripples produced by pebbles dropped in a pool – is the source of inspiration behind this particular form of divination. Usually, but not necessarily the water was contained in a pool dedicated to one or other of the pantheon in which the seer believed.

Icthyomancy

Believers in icthyomancy think that by watching the way a fish behaves when it is placed in a consecrated pool, they, too, can swim in the waters of knowledge of tomorrow.

Lampadomancy

The way that the flames of torches used specifically for lampadomancy flicker allows those who practise this divinatory art to shed light on the events of tomorrow and the days thereafter.

Lecanomancy

Lecanomancers gaze into a basin of water in much the same way that crystallomancers (see above) focus on their crystals hoping that as they reflect on their own or their followers' questions, the answers will be revealed.

Libanomancy

As incense burns, the fumes given off twist and turn in the air, creating endlessly fascinating patterns. It is these patterns that libanomancers observe, hoping to see in them the solutions to whatever it is that troubles them.

Lithomancy

Precious stones have long fascinated humankind, and it is little surprise, therefore, to learn that they were – and still are – used in divination. With their own powers and colours, gemstones can be used by lithomancers to gaze into many aspects of the future.

Margaritomancy

Margaritomancers hold a pearl in their hands, think deeply of the questions they want answered, and drop it on to a solid surface. The way it bounces and how it rolls and comes to rest, give those who seek to know, their insights into the future!

Metagnomy

Many seers fall into a trance during which they have visions of the future. Many clairvoyants do this, as do practitioners of many kinds of divination. Metagnomy is a general term for this divination derived from visions received during a trance.

Meteoromancy

Today, most people (in the western world at least) know that meteors are small pieces of space debris that burn up on entering the Earth's atmosphere and produce shooting stars. Lacking this knowledge, our ancestors regarded them as portents of future events. This belief lingers on, not just in developing lands, meteoromancers believing that these pyrotechnic phenomena can illumine the future.

Metoposcopy

Whereas phrenology (see below) concerns itself with the shape of the skull to give practitioners of the art a head start in future events, metoposcopy considers that the lines of the forehead are what matters when assessing a person's character and hence gaining an insight into what could await the sitter.

Molybdomancy

When lead is heated to liquid form, a loud hissing emanates from the melting pot. According to molybdomancers those who inhabit the spirit world and know what the future holds communicate this knowledge to those in tune with them via this medium.

Myomancy

The manner in which several of the thousands of rats and mice (the most numerous family of all mammals) scurry hither and thither in response to various stimuli tells those who practise myomancy the course of future events. Cynics may say that when they perceive rats leaving a ship, it is pretty obvious that the boat is about to sink! But in parts of the world where people are more in tune with nature than the city sophisticates of the western world, rodent behaviour is regarded as a means of divining the future.

Numerology

One of the best-known methods of divination, numerology divines by interpreting numbers, dates and the numerical value of letters. Numbers were used for divination by the Ancient Chinese and Egyptians, but it was in Classical Greece and among the Hebrews that numerology was developed, Pythagoras, for example, believing that numbers were, 'the first things in Nature'.

Oculomancy

The eyes, it is said, are the keys to the soul. They are also, according to oculomancy, a reliable guide to a person's character and when focused on by a practised oculomancer can provide clues as to what they will behold in the future.

Oenomancy

Wine is not only pleasant to drink, oenomancers believe that when poured into special chalices and gazed into, what they see will uncork future events. It can also be poured from the chalice and the patterns it forms can, to experienced eyes, yield clues to tomorrow's world.

Omphalomancy

This particular method of divination has but one use only – to fore-tell the number of subsequent children women will have by counting the knots on the umbilical cord following the arrival of the firstborn.

Oneiromancy

Dream interpretation's proper name, oneiromancy must be a contender for the oldest form of divination. Maybe the most famous of those with the gift of telling dreamers what their nocturnal imaginings meant is Joseph, whose adventures are related in the Old Testament Book of Genesis. And perhaps the most amusing comment on this was made by Sir Tim Rice who, in the lyrics of Joseph and His Amazing Technicolour Dreamcoat, has Joseph interpreting the Pharaoh's dream in the words, 'All those things you saw in your pyjamas, were the long-range forecast for the farmers.'

Onomancy
Names are the driving force behind this method of divination, which has its roots in numerology (see above). The letters they contain and the syllables they form are ascribed values that combine to enable the seer to plot the course to take.

Onychomancy
This branch of the art of palmistry (see below) concentrates on the fingernails – their shape length and other features – rather than the whole hand, to fulfil its divinatory function. There is a definite scientific base to part of onychomancy as the colour of a person's nails can be indicative of certain conditions: for example, nails that have a hint of yellow about them may suggest liver problems.

Oomantia
Oomantia (also known as ooscopy and ovamancy), is a method of divination that uses eggs rolled on the ground, spun round or simply passed from the hand of those who have questions to the hand of those with answers as its inspiration. The diviner may simply observe the egg, grasp it hoping to feel vibrations, or hold it to his ear.

Opiomancy
The hissing of snakes, the way they move along the ground and respond to what they encounter is the basis of this serpentine method of divination.

Orniscopy
Sometimes known as orinthomancy, this is a branch of apantomancy (see above). It uses the behaviour and movements of birds, particularly those in the air, to enable diviners to take a flight into the future to see

what it holds both for themselves and those who seek to gain from their gifts. Shakespeare mentions divination by this method in The Tragedy of Julius Caesar when he has Casca bid his fellow conspirators to: 'heed...

... the bird of night [that] did sit

Even at noon-day, upon the market-place, hooting and shrieking.'

Palmistry

Experts in this ancient art use the lines, mounds and shape of the hands, fingers and nails as the basis for their assessments of the character and future developments of those having their palm read. The mounds (or mounts) are each linked with one or other of the planets, marrying palmistry and the equally old art of astrology (see above) in happy unison.

Pegomancy

Spring water and the way it bubbles up through natural fountains are used by pegomancers to discern how those who seek the way ahead should take the plunge.

Phrenology

One of the oldest methods of divination, phrenology uses the shape of the head and the small mounds and depression on the skull to give a character reading and to foretell the future of those who want to know what awaits them as they tread their way along the bumpy path of life. However, it is now out of fashion due to the way some historical practitioners connected the practice to their own racist prejudices.

Phyllorhodmancy

This charming method of divining the future involves a rose petal being slapped against the face of the person who would know what will grow in the garden that is the future. The diviner listens carefully for the sound that results from the floral assault and bases his or her auguries on it!

Physiognomy

Practitioners of this art study the physical features of the faces of those who seek their wisdom to analyze their characters, which, some believe, may provide a pointer to what is in store.

Physchography

Physchographers are in tune with a spiritual force that 'tells' those blessed with the gift messages to write down, sometimes but not always, when the seer is in a trance. There are many recorded cases of this 'automatic writing' including several whereby dead composers have used the medium of a living person as the chalice whereby they can carry on their work from beyond the grave.

Pyramancy

Also known as pyroscopy, pyramancy is a general term for divining the future by studying fire and flame. Divination is often assisted by throwing substances onto the flames (see also botanomancy, capnomancy, causiomancy, daphamancy, lampadomancy and libanomancy, and xylomancy).

Radiesthesia

This is a general term for divination that uses a device such as a divining rod or pendulum.

Rhapsodomancy

This rather romantic method of divination uses poetry as its inspiration. Those with the gift of rhapsodamancy use a book of verse opened at random and a chance-chosen passage on that page as their way of divining future chapters in life's tome. The practice is a branch of stichomancy (see below) and bibliomancy (see above).

Sciomancy

Sciomancers are mediums by another name – people with the gift of communicating with the spirit guides who inhabit the unseen world, usually when in a trance-like state.

Scrying

Whole books have been written about scrying, an all-encompassing term for divination via a wide of assortment of aids from smoke to shells to induce visions that tell what the gods have in store for us.

Sideromancy

This rare, but still-practised form of divination is, like so many, pagan in origin. Sideromancers use a hot iron to set straw a-smouldering, and study the various shapes the stalks adopt as they slowly catch fire. They also consider the way any smoke given off twists and spirals upwards, interpreting what they see through the haze to give them insights into tomorrow's world.

Sortilege

Those who practise sortilege cast lots and use the shapes in which they fall as the basis of their omens. The lots can take several forms – animal, vegetable and mineral. There are many versions of sortilege, which have been given their own names.

Spodomancy

Our ancient ancestors understandably held fire in some awe. They used it to heat their primitive dwellings, cook their food and guard them from marauding animals. It is little wonder then that fire is involved in some way in so many forms of divination. This particular one involves deciphering the patterns seen in cinders and soot to peer into tomorrow.

Stichomancy

A branch of divination that, like rhapsodomancy, uses the printed word to turn pages of the upcoming chapters in the Book of Life. But whereas the latter relies on poetry, stichomancy can be done with any book (see also Bibliomancy).

Stolisomancy

This curious (but perhaps no more curious than others) method of telling the future considers that the way people dress holds the clue not just to their character, but also to their future. There is probably something in the argument that what one chooses to wear in the morning does reflect the way one feels, and wearing certain colours might affect one's mood, so perhaps this particular form of divination should be regarded with more respect than it is in some quarters.

Sycomancy

This sylvan form of divination is performed by writing various prophecies or different answers to the same question on tree leaves, and leaving them to dry naturally. Whatever is written on the last leaf to dry is most likely to come true. A more modern version requires those seeking what they wish for the future to write their desires on slips of paper which are then rolled up and, along with one blank rolled piece, put in a strainer and held over a boiling pot. The first to unroll is, it is believed, the wish that will come true. If the blank one unrolls before the others it is a warning that there is no point in proceeding with the divination at this particular moment in time.

Tasseography

Reading the leaves is one of the most popular forms of amateur divination. After the tea has been enjoyed, the cup is placed upside down on the saucer to drain it completely, and the shapes formed by the leaves are interpreted as pointers to the way things will be. The origins of reading the leaves are obscure, but it is known to have been practised in China for thousands of years, which is hardly surprising as tea-drinking was common there for many millennia before it spread to other countries.

Tiromancy

Cheese and the crumbs it leaves on the plate may seem unlikely pointers to the future, but in the world of divination, there is little that cannot be used as indicative of things to come – and what's on the cheeseboard or growing on the cheese is no exception.

Xylomancy

The shapes of pieces of wood when they are collected and the way this changes when the logs are burned is the basis on which xylomancers make their predictions as to how to cope with any future knotty problems (see pyromancy above).

In an ideal world, each one of these different methods of divination would be given equal space. We would look at the history of them all, where they were or still are practised, and how effective they are. Sadly, we don't live in an ideal world. Instead, we will concentrate on the ones with which most of us have come in contact, or which are accessible to us.

Cynics will say that divination in these and its other myriad forms is a load of pie in the sky: everyone is entitled to their own opinion. But others, perhaps more open-minded souls, will pause for a moment before they join the ranks of the disbelievers. They would be wise to do so, for there is a considerable body of evidence in favour of those who are certain that there is something in it.

Of course, no one (at least no one sensible) would claim that the old lady who sets up a stall at the vicar's fête and charges good-natured villagers a pound to peer into her crystal ball and tell their future is doing anything else than raising some much-needed cash for the restoration fund. And when she has a friend round for tea and offers to 'read your cup, dear,' no one really believes that she has 'the gift'. But what about the well-documented case of the seven-year-old girl whose mother slept during the day and kept watch all night when sailing on a cross-Atlantic liner because she 'knew' it was going to sink? The mother was called Esther and young girl's name was Eva Hart… and the ship was the RMS Titanic.

Or Jeanne Dixon, one of the United States' most celebrated clairvoyants. In 1956 she foretold that a Democratic president with 'thick brown hair and blue eyes', would be assassinated by a man whose name began with O or Q. Seven years later, John F. Kennedy was assassinated in Texas by a man whose name began with an O – Lee Harvey Oswald.

As Hamlet said, 'There are more things in heaven and earth, Horatio, than are dreamt of in your philosophy.' Successful divination is one of them.

1

TAROT

THE TAROT UNLOCKS in the psyche messages from a vast mysterious universe, one that may in fact be psychologically located in one's own subconscious. Modern tarot readers do not ask for their palms to be crossed with silver while they pronounce the swift arrival of a tall, handsome stranger. They are as likely to advise you on how to approach forthcoming challenges as they are to prophesize about what is due to happen to you.

The tarot's universal symbols speak of a journey; it is the one we all embark upon at birth and it is our own personal heroic path through life. So, even if you are sceptical about the power of the tarot cards to predict the future, there is much to recommend them as a guide to discovering what concerns you have lying just under the surface of your consciousness.

Some of the imagery of the deck can be worrying – the figure of Death cutting down souls or people falling headlong from a blazing tower – however, this should be considered in the manner of a dream after you awake. You will not die (or at least not immediately after drawing a Death card) and you are unlikely to plummet from a high vantage point either. The Death in the card is one necessary for transformation and change to come about and the people falling from the Tower are losing their long-held, manmade beliefs represented by the tower in the picture.

As you do a reading, remember that your fate is not predetermined and outcomes will change as you change your attitude, behaviour and responses. A reading is a snapshot of what is coming in the next 6-12 months for you and it is rare that a reader will be able to accurately draw cards for any longer period of time than that.

History of the Tarot

The origins of the tarot are not known, but evidence suggests that the cards as we recognise them have been in existence since the fifteenth century. The first set of Tarot cards we know of, the Visconti-Sforza pack, is Italian in origin; the second and more complete set is known as the Charles VI pack, named after the king of France at the time, although this deck may also have originated in Italy. The earliest evidence of playing cards in existence dates back to ninth century China, so it may be that medieval Tarot cards were based on these earlier playing cards.

Tarot cards are thought to have been used in card games known as *tarocchi*. The only firm evidence we have that they were used to divine the future dates from the eighteenth century, although there is fragmentary evidence to show they may have been used for this purpose much earlier.

The symbolic images on the Tarot cards reflect the medieval and Renaissance European cultures from which they emerged. There were many multicultural influences in Renaissance Europe, including hermetic thought from ancient Egypt and Greece and other divination systems such as astrology and the kabbalah. All these belief systems would have had followers at the time and the images on the Tarot reflect this. However, although the cards are clearly rooted in the ancient past, there is a timeless quality to the symbolism that speaks to people across cultures today and ensures their continued popularity.

HOW TO USE THE CARDS

The choice of decks

Today there are hundreds of different Tarot designs to choose from, many of which have a theme or specific purpose, such as answering questions about love and romantic relationships or catering to every interest, from pets to Arthurian legends. Given the wide range of choice, it can be difficult for the beginner to decide which type to select. Ideally we inherit our cards from a relative or friend, but many of us buy our own packs and let our instincts guide us.

Interpretations often allude to the symbols found in one of the most popular sets of Tarot cards – the Rider-Waite-Smith pack. Created in 1909, it was designed by artist Pamela Colman Smith according to the instructions of Arthur Edward Waite – an academic, freemason and prominent member of the Hermetic Order of the Golden Dawn (a group similar to a masonic order, but interested in magical and occult theory) – and produced by the Rider company. Originally called the Rider-Waite pack (but amended to include Smith's contribution), it is now the standard deck and has been used as a template for numerous others. For this reason, we will look in detail at the meaning of the cards in this popular deck later in this section. Each card has its own meaning, which is applied to the context of the question being asked as well as to the card's particular position in a spread.

When learning the Tarot, it is advisable to understand the meaning of the cards and then develop your own personal interpretation as you become more proficient. In this way, you develop your own intuitive system. You may also want to create your own deck of Tarot cards and personalise them by using the images you associate with the meaning of the cards.

The Minor and Major Arcana

The Tarot deck is comprised of 78 cards, 56 of which are divided into four suits and known as the Minor Arcana. The remaining 22 are picture cards known as the Major Arcana. Arcana is a Latin word meaning 'secret', 'mystery' or 'mysterious' and refers to the mysteries the Tarot helps us to uncover.

The Minor Arcana cards correspond with the suits in ordinary playing cards and with the four elements of fire, earth, air and water as well as representing other esoteric qualities (see the Table of Correspondence below). The Major Arcana cards are not thought to correspond with playing cards. They are often numbered from 0-21, although the order varies slightly depending on the deck being used. They usually follow from the Fool card at 0 through to the World at 21.

TABLE OF CORRESPONDENCE OF THE MINOR ARCANA

Tarot suit	Playing card suit	Element	Season	Timing	Qualities
Wands	Clubs	Fire	Spring	Days	Action, creativity, energy, enterprise, intuition, hope, potential
Cups	Hearts	Water	Summer	Months	Love, relationships, happiness, harmony, sensitivity, emotion, fulfillment
Swords	Spades	Air	Autumn	Weeks	Ideas, communication, conflict, struggle, separation, resolution, change
Pentacle	Diamonds	Earth	Winter	Years	Money, work, talent, reputation, achievement, stability, material realm

The suits

In a standard Tarot deck, the Minor Arcana has four suits, each of which corresponds to a playing cards suit – the wands or batons (clubs), cups or chalices (hearts), swords (spades) and pentacles or coins (diamonds).

There are four sets of cards in each suit and they are numbered 1-10, with the ace as the first card. There are also court cards in each suit, although the Tarot has one extra court card – the Tarot knight.

The court cards

There are sixteen court cards in the Tarot pack; each of the four suits has a king, a queen, a knight and a page. If a court card appears in a spread, it may represent an individual in your life who possesses the card's particular attributes. However, it can also represent qualities of the querent which need to find expression. The kings represent mature male authority figures who embody power, paternalism, achievement and responsibility. Queens are mature, maternal females and, like the kings, figures of authority. They embody wisdom, confidence, fertility and life-giving qualities. Knights are immature men and women who are rash in their actions and tend to pursue their own desires and interests at the expense of others. Knights indicate change and movement in a new direction. Pages refer to children or young teenagers of either gender and represent youthful potential, dreams and other characteristics that are hard to define. The qualities they embody are delicate and need to be nurtured if they are to develop. Pages are messengers and indicate that news of some kind will be received.

Elements and qualities

The card suits also correspond to the four esoteric elements of earth, air, fire and water and their associated qualities (see Table of Correspondence opposite).

Timing with Tarot cards

If a particular suit is dominant in a spread it may indicate when an event is likely to happen. The wands correspond with springtime and action, so represent the fastest unit of time (days); the cups correspond with summer and represent weeks; the swords correspond with autumn and represent months; and the pentacles correspond with winter and represent a year.

Care of the Cards

Everyone handles their cards in their own way, but part of the ritual and etiquette of using a Tarot deck is to treat it with care. Practitioners are advised to keep the cards clean and wrapped in a cloth, pouch or placed in a box and stored in a private place when not in use.

It is advisable to become familiar with your cards and handle them regularly to build up a connection with them. In general, only the owner of the cards should handle them. In this way, you develop a deeper connection and when you come to consult the cards it is like approaching a personal confidante for advice. If you give a reading to another person (known as the querent), you may ask him or her to shuffle or cut the deck, but the querent's contact with the cards should be kept to a minimum.

Preparing the cards for a reading

Before the cards are laid out, they must be shuffled. It is worth focusing your mind on the question asked by the querent while you shuffle the cards. Then cut the deck once or three times and lay it out according to one of the spreads. Alternatively you can fan the deck out on a table and draw the number of cards required at random, placing each one in its position in the spread in the order you pick them. Some Tarot readers leave the cards face down and turn each one over as they come to them during the reading. Card readings can also be given using only the Major Arcana. The reader needs to separate these cards from the rest of the pack and shuffle them as normal.

General indications

When many cards of the same suit turn up in a spread, it could show that a particular element or quality is influencing the matter. If Major

Arcana cards predominate, it may suggest there are wider forces at work and that external factors will determine the matter. When mostly Minor Arcana cards appear, it may suggest that the matter is in the querent's hands. Aces represent new beginnings and, depending on their position in a spread, may indicate that the answer to a question is 'Yes'. The court cards may represent people in our lives who have the qualities ascribed to the cards, or they may direct our attention to those qualities in ourselves.

Tips when reading the cards

The Tarot is a complex system of divination. As with other forms of divination, on a superficial level it is just another form of fortune-telling. However, the cards have a deeper significance than mere prediction because they offer insights into the forces that are work in your life and within your innermost self.

We should remember to approach the reading with humility, compassion and sensitive consideration for all involved – including ourselves, the querent and anyone else who crops up in the question or during the course of the reading.

The symbols should also be treated with care and used to help both reader and querent gain insights that will be of benefit. Whatever the nature of the cards selected, the reading should never end on a negative note. If the outcome is undesirable, we need to take the advice of the cards and consider how we can work towards a better outcome. Sometimes the cards may indicate that our desire for certain things will not lead to the best outcome for ourselves. It may take repeated readings, with the same results, before we understand and accept this message. Sometimes the Tarot can play up and will appear to give readings that don't seem relevant to the question posed. In these cases it is best to leave the cards for a while and start the reading afresh later on. You have to work hard to get the most out of the Tarot, but remember that words are no substitute for experience and being guided by others is no substitute for using your own instincts. Surrender to them and you will be richly rewarded.

Reversed cards

When cards are reversed in a spread, they can be interpreted as having the opposite meaning to the one they have when upright. However, some people only use the upright meanings of the cards. These are the meanings we will use here.

Selecting a significator

A card can be selected to signify yourself, the querent and any other individual who may crop up in the reading. This card is called a significator, or signifier, and is usually the court card (page, knight, queen, king) which best describes the appearance and characteristics of the person in question.

The querent's astrological Sun sign may be taken into consideration when selecting the significator. For example, if the querent is female and her Sun is in an earth sign (Taurus, Virgo or Capricorn), then the Queen of Pentacles may be chosen to represent her – particularly if she also possesses the characteristics of that card, such as generosity, practical talents and a strong connection with nature and the physical world. If not, then another card may suit her better and this can be chosen as her significator instead.

The significator can be taken out of the deck and placed in the centre of a spread, or next to the spread, to set the tone and provide a focus for the reading. Alternatively, the significator can be left in the deck; if the querent's significator then appears in the spread, it can be understood to represent him or her in the reading or the qualities he or she embodies.

Tarot spreads

A single card may be selected from the deck to answer a question, to provide general guidance on present events or serve as a focus for meditation. Alternatively, one of the following spreads can be used to answer a question or give a general reading. There are many different ways to lay out the cards in preparation for a reading.

The three-card spread

One of the simplest layouts is the three-card spread. The first card is selected and placed face up – this represents the past. The second card is taken and placed on the right of the first card – this represents the present. The third card is placed to the right of the others – this represents the future.

Sample reading using the three-card spread

The querent is a young female in her early twenties. She has raised a question pertaining to a relationship that has failed. She is asking the cards to shed light on the situation and bring guidance to help her move on from the heartbreak and give an idea of what the future might hold. The querent has selected the following cards:

Card 1: the past

This is represented by the Lovers card, which describes the experience of a deep connection with another person in the past. One might surmise that this was an important relationship that has had a strong effect on both people's lives. They may have felt they had made the right match. It would not be surprising if such a connection was difficult and painful to lose.

Card 2: the present

The Sun in this position suggests that the most important focus for the querent at present is herself and her own healing. Perhaps the relationship has awakened her self-confidence and creativity. She should concentrate on her creative potential right now and find joy and satisfaction through achieving her own goals and potential. In this way she will gradually heal the wounds of heartbreak and regain a connection with the self that may have been lost or compromised in a relationship with another.

Card 3: the future
The Hierophant in this position indicates that the experience of the relationship has led to a growth in wisdom and maturity. A new perspective on the matter will be found. A lesson will be learnt and will result in the development of a new personal philosophy and outlook on life. It may lead the querent to take a course of study or learn a new skill which will bring greater personal fulfilment.

Since all three cards are from the Major Arcana, we can surmise that greater forces are at work and the matter is out of the querent's hands. Perhaps the failed relationship was inevitable in some way – the two individuals were destined to meet, but the results of meeting and being forced to separate will lead to necessary changes in the querent's life.

The relationship spread
This is a useful spread for interpreting your relationship to another person, be that your partner, your boss, a family member or friend. The cards are laid out as opposite. Since it is a spread for the relationship between two people, make sure you keep the person in mind as you are shuffling and don't muddy the waters by thinking too much about the situation at hand. You may even find that what you thought was going on between you and the other person is the direct opposite, as in the case when someone is being aloof with you but secretly rather likes you.

1   What you think of the other person
2   What they think of you
3   The strengths in the relationship

4   The obstacles in the relationship
5   Where you are right now
6   What influences are likely to come into play
7   The final outcome

1   The Emperor
2   Queen of Swords
3   The Devil
4   The Star
5   The Empress
6   Ace of Cups
7   Two of swords

Sample reading using the relationship spread
A woman wishes to know where she stands with a longstanding on-off relationship with a man she knows.

1. What you think of the other person

The Emperor here indicates that she feels he can be a bit domineering and arrogant and attempts to railroad her into accepting elements of the relationship on his terms. This is not to say that she doesn't think well of him as the Emperor is a born leader and can be charismatic and attractive.

2. What they think of you

Interestingly, the character of the Queen of Swords can be quite similar to that of the Emperor – she is analytical, strong and is brutally honest. This card in this position does show that he is attracted to her humour and her integrity, but the problems may like in how similar the two are to each other.

3. The strengths in the relationship

The Devil in this position shows a degree of eroticism in the relationship that is healthy and strong. The two are clearly attracted to each other physically and this aspect of the relationship is often what draws them back together.

4. The obstacles in the relationship

Alas there are too many hopes and expectations placed on the relationship, whether by the querent or the man she is asking about. This desire to have the relationship be what it isn't is blocking progress and frustrating each partner.

5. Where you are right now

The Empress card can often indicate a woman who is loved and content in that love, which is odd as the querent is clearly not content or secure in her relationship with this man. It could be that this is another woman in the man's life. It is also a card of fertility and may show an unexpected pregnancy.

6. What influences are likely to come into play

An Ace of Cups here reinforces the news of a baby. It is good here to check cards in the position before and after to see if it is a baby between the two people in the query or between one of the people and someone else. It seems likely here that the man has another relationship that will result in a child.

7. The final outcome
The Two of Swords is a card of self-defensiveness and of blindly fighting your corner. It seems as though this relationship is likely to hit some bumps and one of those might be a pregnancy one!

The horseshoe spread
In this spread, seven cards are laid out in a horseshoe shape (see page 42). This spread is helpful if the querent has a particular question in mind or it can be used to give a general reading of current circumstances.

The meanings of each card position are as follows:

1   The past
2   The present
3   Hidden influences
4   Obstacles that must be overcome
5   Others' perspectives
6   The best path to take
7   The final outcome

1   Three of Pentacles
2   King of Swords
3   The Empress
4   Six of Pentacles
5   The Hermit
6   The Hierophant
7   The Ace of Pentacles

Sample reading using the horseshoe spread
A young man asked to have a general reading and selected the seven cards shown overleaf.

1. The past

The Three of Pentacles in this position indicates that the querent has been working hard and learning a trade of some kind. He has proven his skills and abilities to others and been recognized for his achievements in some way. Perhaps he has been trying to work out which direction to take with his career.

2. The present

The King of Swords in this position suggests that the querent is in a strong position of authority at this time. Perhaps his mental and analytical skills are being put to good use in his work as well as his private life. Or he may be in a particularly rational state of mind, able to think his options through and weigh them up to make the right decisions. He may be called upon to help others do the same. Being a court card, the King of Swords may also represent someone in the querent's life who displays these qualities and has an influence over the querent.

3. Hidden influences

The Empress in this position implies that a feminine figure has a hidden influence over the querent's life at the moment. Such a card may represent his mother or another female in his life. She is working for his benefit behind the scenes, trying to steer him in the right direction without his knowledge and only wants the best for him.

4. Obstacles that must be overcome

The Six of Pentacles in this position may indicate that the querent's wish to share his wealth with others is holding him back in some way. Perhaps he needs to be careful with his resources and save for his future.

5. Others' perspectives

The Hermit in this position suggests that others may be thinking the querent is difficult to reach at the moment. He seems to have retreated from his normal activities and relationships to take time to think about his life and where he is going. He doesn't seem to have much time for his loved ones and they are no doubt looking forward to hearing from him!

6. The best path to take

The Hierophant in this position suggests that the querent needs to work out what is meaningful and important to him. Perhaps he will seek advice from a wise counsellor who can help to steer him on the right path. The querent has many questions about his meaning and purpose in life and may need to take some time to get in touch with his thoughts.

7. The final outcome

The Ace of Pentacles signifies that the final outcome will be the start of new business projects and ventures. Perhaps the card points to the setting up of a new business or to a job offer that is just what the querent was looking for. The purchase of a home, a sense of security and material comforts may also be indicated.

There are a number of pentacles in the spread, suggesting that career and financial matters are uppermost among the querent's concerns at the moment. Equally, the high number of Major Arcana cards suggests that there is a higher purpose at work; the querent can therefore trust that his path will unfold as it should.

The Celtic cross spread

The Celtic cross is one of the most widely used Tarot spreads today, covering general themes and providing a snapshot of a particular matter. In this spread, ten cards are laid out in the shape of a cross and a staff (see opposite).

The meanings of each card position are:

1. The querent (a significator card can be selected for the querent and used in this position or a card can be picked at random)
2. The obstacle or influences that have a bearing on the question
3. The question itself and the basis of the matter
4. The recent past – something that has just happened that has a direct influence on the question
5. The highest potential of the matter
6. The near future in relation to the question
7. Fears and concerns that the querent has about the matter
8. Other people's perspectives – how other people see the situation
9. The querent's hopes and wishes for the future outcome
10. The overall outcome of the matter

Sample reading using the Celtic cross spread

The querent is a man in his mid-thirties. He has asked whether he should buy a property, but is unsure if he should take on the responsibility of a mortgage at the moment.

1. The querent

A card was picked at random from the pack to represent the querent in the first position. The card selected was the Devil. This does not suggest that the querent is evil! It means that he has his own interests

at heart and will put his needs first in this matter. It may indicate that finding shelter is a matter of urgency and the querent may find himself homeless unless the situation is resolved quickly.

2. The obstacle or influences that have a bearing on the question

The Two of Wands in this position suggests a lot of work and effort has gone into searching for the right home and that the querent has now stopped to take stock. Perhaps he finds himself unable to move forward to make the decision and close the deal.

3. The question itself and the basis of the matter

The Seven of Pentacles in this position reinforces the suggestion that the querent is tired and weary after a period of hard work and research into buying a home. This may be deterring him from going ahead with buying a property. He is advised to stop for a rest and take stock of the matter before moving forward.

4. The recent past – an event that has a direct influence on the question

The Ten of Pentacles in this position suggests that material wealth and stability have been achieved. Perhaps the querent has saved enough money or received an inheritance that makes it possible to purchase a property. A great store of personal resources is indicated by this card.

5. The highest potential of the matter

The Page of Wands in the position of the highest potential represents a creative spirit who calls for excitement and adventure. This card may represent the querent's own creative potential or it could be someone else who has influence in the matter. This card suggests that the querent's priority is not to get tied down in one place but to maintain a carefree lifestyle. For this reason, it does not look likely that the client will be purchasing the property at the moment.

6. The near future in relation to the question

The Five of Cups in this position suggests that the client's dreams and wishes may be dashed. Perhaps the opportunity to buy the property he has set his heart on will be lost and disappointment will follow. Or perhaps a relationship problem or break-up will affect his decision.

7. Fears and concerns the querent has about the matter

The Six of Wands in this position suggests that the querent is afraid of success! Everything he wants is within his grasp but this may be causing such anxiety that he is unable to move forward. The querent should consider why he fears the possibility of achieving everything he set out to do. This card, together with the placement of the 5th card, suggests that perhaps he is frightened of the responsibilities that come with success.

8. Other people's perspectives – how other people see the situation

The World in this position suggests that other people think the world is the querent's oyster! They may believe he is in the enviable position of being able to do whatever he pleases and that limitless opportunities are open to him. Other people's opinions may be encouraging him to act cautiously to ensure he is not squandering the opportunities available to him.

9. The querent's hopes and wishes for the future outcome

The King of Wands in this position suggests that the querent has high aspirations. He dreams of travelling and seeing the world before settling down. The querent should follow his intuition and take the path that helps him to realize his dreams and achieve his greatest potential.

10. The overall outcome of the matter

The Six of Pentacles in this position indicates that after achieving his dreams the client will be able to share his wealth and success with others. While his wealth may diminish slightly (it was the Ten of Pentacles in the past, now it has been reduced to the Six of Pentacles), he will find a way to use his resources for the benefit of all.

The majority of cards in this reading are wands, followed by pentacles, which means that freedom and discovery take priority over settling down into a stable routine. After the heartache that may be on its way in the near future (indicated by the 6th card placement), the querent will be free to pursue his dreams and should follow his intuition in making decisions about the future.

The astrological spread

The astrological spread is based on the twelve houses of the Zodiac. It is laid out in the shape of a circular horoscope, with one card chosen to represent each of the twelve houses. If we compare the horoscope to a clock face, the first card is laid at nine o'clock, the second at eight o'clock and so on, in an anti-clockwise direction, with the twelfth card at ten o'clock. This spread is often used to get a snapshot of the querent's life at the moment and can answer questions about various aspects, such as relationships and career.

The areas of life covered by each card position are as follows:

1 The querent's appearance and persona
2 Personal values and monetary matters
3 Communications and short journeys
4 Home and family
5 Romance, creativity and children
6 Work and health
7 Relationships and business partnerships
8 Shared resources, inheritance and secrets
9 Teaching, learning and long journeys
10 Vocation, career goals and aspirations
11 Friends, groups and community
12 Unconscious and hidden realm

1 Eight of Pentacles
2 Nine of Cups
3 Ace of Cups
4 Eight of Cups
5 Seven of Cups
6 The Emperor
7 Knight of Wands
8 Page of Pentacles
9 Five of Wands
10 Ace of Pentacles
11 Strength
12 Ace of Wands

Sample reading using the astrological spread

The querent is a female in her early forties who would like a general reading about relationships and career matters. We can look to the 5th and 7th house positions in particular to describe relationships, and the 2nd, 6th and 10th houses for an indication of career prospects, although all the cards have a bearing on the chart. We should also look at each house position to get a general picture of a person's current experiences.

The querent has selected the following cards:

1. The querent's appearance and persona

The Eight of Pentacles in this position suggests that the querent is working hard to achieve her goals and perhaps training and learning new skills. To others, she might seem consumed by work at the moment and very serious about her career.

2. Personal values and monetary matters

The Nine of Cups in this position indicates that great wealth and emotional security are possible. Work is extremely satisfying and rewarding. If this does not describe the querent's current job, it should do so in the near future if the querent continues on her current path.

3. Communications and short journeys

The Ace of Cups in this position describes the ability to communicate with others from the heart. A new friendship or romance may begin as the result of a chance meeting while on a short journey. A love letter may be on its way.

4. Home and family

The Eight of Cups in this position suggests that the querent needs some time away from her home and family to gain some perspective and learn to appreciate them again. It also indicates that it might be helpful for the querent to explore her family background and roots.

5. Romance, creativity and children

The Seven of Cups in this position points to the need to make a decision regarding a lover. If it is relevant, there may be a choice involving children. The querent may be feeling creative at this time and should listen to messages arising out of the imagination and dreams to help her come to a decision.

6. Work and health

The Emperor in this position suggests that a decision needs to be made about the querent's job. This could involve taking on increased responsibilities as well as the wider decision about what job the querent really wants to be doing. The Emperor card recommends self-discipline and suggests that a father figure may have influence over the querent's decisions. The querent should make sure she fulfils her responsibilities at work and maintains a good healthcare regime.

7. Relationships and business partnerships

The Knight of Wands in this position represents a current partner or person about to enter the querent's life, who is fiery, courageous and brash. Perhaps the querent has had an argument with her partner that has resulted in angry scenes and caused her to question the relationship. The card might also signify that the querent's love life is about to take a new direction.

8. Shared resources, inheritance and secrets

The Page of Pentacles in this position indicates that the querent is being sensible with money and in matters that have been entrusted to her. She may be relied upon to keep a secret. In this placement, the card also suggests the querent has inherited a sense of responsibility and strong work ethic from her parents.

9. Teaching, learning and long journeys

The Five of Wands in this position suggests a crisis in the querent's personal philosophies and beliefs. Perhaps the fiery arguments with her partner stem from this. The querent may need to visit a conflict zone or she may be met with hostility when travelling to a distant location. As indicated by the 1st card in the spread, she is currently working to develop a new skill but may encounter obstacles that impact on her learning. The problem needs to be addressed head on and a resolution found.

10. Vocation, career goals and aspirations

The Ace of Pentacles in this position represents great material rewards and achievements in the querent's career and chosen profession. Perhaps a new job opportunity or business venture is imminent. This placement indicates that the querent is on the right track to achieve her career goals and ambitions. Her hard work and diligence will pay off.

11. Friends, groups and community

The Strength card in this position shows that the querent is regarded highly by her friends and wider community. While she encounters conflict in other parts of her life, the querent is in a strong position to work for the benefit of those around her and may be asked to defend friends who are in need of assistance.

12. Unconscious and hidden realm

The Ace of Wands in this position is an interesting placement for such a lively and active card. It could suggest that the querent's intuition is particularly strong at this time and she should use it to navigate the way ahead. She may also need to explore her anger, which may be rumbling beneath the surface and could be a reason for the conflicts encountered in her relationships.

Overall, there are mostly cups and pentacles in this reading, reflecting the focus of the question which was on relationships (cups) and career matters (pentacles). It looks as though important decisions need to be made in both areas and that the querent has the diligence and commitment to succeed along whichever path she chooses.

THE MAJOR ARCANA –
The Fool's Journey

0 The Fool

'I embark on my journey with trust and a light heart for the world opens up before me…'

Keywords: fresh start, beginning, freedom, courage, openness, trust, risk-taking

The Fool is shown standing on the edge of a precipice, bag and rose in hand, with a dog at his heels. He is stepping into the unknown, alone except for his trusty dog, full of expectation and potential and unfettered by the doubts and cynicism that come with experience. The card suggests a choice must be made and a journey started into unknown territory. Courage is required to take the first step. The Fool is unaware of and unprepared for what awaits him, but through new experiences will discover his true potential.

1 The Magician

'I am the master of my destiny and hold all the keys to success…'

Keywords: skills, potential, mastery, resourcefulness, will, power, creativity, action

The Magician stands next to a table upon which lie a wand, a sword, a chalice and a pentacle. These represent the four Tarot suits and the four elements. Wand in hand, the Magician is about use his powers to command his will. Above his head the infinity symbol, known as the cosmic lemniscate, represents the eternal and immortal force of energy. At this first stage of his journey, the Fool realizes that he has all the resources he needs to gain mastery over the material world of opposites and duality. The Magician is an authority figure who has the power to do good. Creativity and resourcefulness are needed to overcome obstacles.

2 The High Priestess

'I am the seer who stands between worlds and makes manifest the unmanifest...'

Keywords: wisdom, intuition, mystery, secrets, hidden knowledge, unseen influences at work

The High Priestess is also described as the veiled Isis. She is seated between two pillars which represent the great universal principles and mark the entrance to the sacred temple. She holds a scroll containing esoteric knowledge on her lap. On her forehead she wears the symbol of the phases of the Moon, representing the cycles of life and the creative force of the female. She stands for hidden knowledge, wisdom and intuition. When she appears in a spread it could indicate that some hidden forces are at work in a situation and one must look inwards for the answer.

3 The Empress

'I am the loved and content woman, full in her power to give and receive love...'

Keywords: abundance, pleasure, contentment, creativity, nature, nurture, balance, fullness, fertility, renewal

The Empress is Isis unveiled. Seated on her throne, she radiates the beauty that comes from harmony with nature. She is the great Earth Mother, in charge of the seasons, the fertility of the soil and production of the food which sustains us. At this stage of the journey, the Fool realizes that he needs to look after his health and physical needs.

The Empress indicates the possibility of marriage and motherhood as well as material gain. With careful attention and nurturing, a creative project will bear fruit. A situation is full of promise and has great potential.

4 The Emperor

'I am the responsible leader who always knows the right action to take...'

Keywords: judgement, decision, action, responsibility, challenge, effectiveness, satisfaction from achievement

The Emperor is the card of fathering and indicates focus and the energy of accomplishment. The Emperor challenges the Fool to build something lasting to be proud of. The Fool is asked to make a decision about what he wants and what he values most in the world. He must then set out to achieve his goal. It will require hard work and unwavering determination and he will be judged on his abilities and the way in which he exercises responsibility. When this card is drawn, someone in a position of authority may offer advice that should be taken seriously.

5 The Hierophant

'I am wisdom in all its forms;
heed me and prosper...'

Keywords: law, tradition, religion, meaning, philosophy, teaching, learning, vision

Also called the High Priest or Pope, the Hierophant is a wise teacher, priest or counsellor to whom we may turn at times of personal crisis. Like the High Priestess, the Hierophant is seated between two pillars at the entrance of the temple. However, unlike the High Priestess, the Hierophant represents the outer trappings and traditions of religious practice. At this stage in his journey the Fool must find meaning and seek answers to questions about the purpose of his life. When this card appears in a spread it indicates that we may be searching for meaning and need to approach a situation with a philosophical outlook.

6 The Lovers

'I will take you to the place of choice where decisions must be made for good or ill…'

Keywords: love, connection, sexual attraction, union of opposites, new possibilities, temptation, choice

In the card of the Lovers, we find a naked man and woman standing next to (and, in some versions, embracing) each other, with the man looking at the woman. The woman is looking up to the sky, where Cupid is watching. The card alludes to the first lovers of the Old Testament – Adam and Eve in the Garden of Eden. Thus, along with love, relationship and the family, the card of the Lovers has come to represent temptation and the need to make a choice. At this stage of his journey, the Fool finds his match and decides to marry and unite the opposites within. The card suggests that a union is possible and there is hope for a bright future ahead.

7 The Chariot

'I am the Charioteer who will guide you to your goal…'

Keywords: action, control, focus, strength, stability, willpower, conflict, struggle, change, triumph

The Chariot card represents gaining control over conflicting forces. The charioteer in the card is trying to control the two sphinxes which are pulling the chariot. The sphinxes – one black, one white – represent principles pulling in opposite directions. The opposites that were united in the previous Lovers card must now be kept moving in the same direction. At this stage in his journey, the Fool must use all his strength to keep on the right track. By seeing what has to be done and taking control of the situation, obstacles will be overcome. If we manage to keep the opposite forces on the same path, we will go far. Events are moving quickly.

8 Strength

'I am the courage you didn't know you possessed...'

Keywords: strength, control, confidence, balance, integrity, courage, generosity, compassion

The card of Strength depicts a woman holding open (or forcing closed) the jaws of a lion, apparently without fear of danger. The lion represents our primal urges, the wild and ravenous beast within, yet the woman has succeeded in taming them. Like the Magician, she has an infinity symbol, or cosmic leminiscate, above her head, indicating that she has achieved a new level of consciousness and understanding. The Fool is gaining mastery over the primal forces that have governed him and his conscious ego is taking control. The card suggests that struggles may be ahead, but we have the courage and confidence to overcome any danger.

9 The Hermit

'I walk the solitary path to find my way through to enlightenment...'

Keywords: solitude, withdrawal, detachment, caution, patience, prudence, discretion, limitation

The Hermit stands alone on a mountaintop, holding up a lamp to light his way. He is wearing a cloak and carrying a staff to help him through the tough terrain. He has retreated from society to gain some perspective and look inward for answers. Through patient searching, he gains insight and connects with his intuitive knowledge. The Fool has reached maturity and questions his direction in life. When the Hermit appears in a spread, we may need to retreat from a situation so that we can recharge our batteries and have space to think. We are advised to retreat and work out what is important to us before taking any further action in a matter.

10 Wheel of Fortune

'I am constantly turning so that which is low will rise again and that which is high will fall...'

Keywords: luck, chance, fortune, destiny, change, success, new direction

The Wheel of Fortune represents an unexpected element that will change the outcome of a matter. It may be good or bad, but generally indicates a turn of luck for the better and may herald opportunities and a new phase in life. Although we are responsible for shaping our own lives, this card suggests that luck and fortune may come along at any moment and change things for the better. When the Wheel of Fortune is drawn, an unexpected solution to a problem may present itself. Sometimes the card reminds us that 'what goes around comes around', and that past actions will be rewarded.

11 Justice

'I am balance that comes with fair reckoning...'

Keywords: fairness, impartiality, balance, reflection, decision, equality, truth

Like the High Priestess and Hierophant, justice is seated between two pillars, suggesting a religious connection. Justice is one of the universal principles upon which society is built. The figure in the card holds a sword and points it upwards, indicating that justice will be upheld. The sword of justice is famously double-edged, however and a balance must be found between two opposing sides for there to be a fair outcome. Following the Wheel of Fortune card, Justice reminds us that we are accountable for our actions and urges us to be honest and fair. This card indicates that justice will prevail.

12 The Hanged Man

'I am the sacrifice we must all make to arrive at the truth…'

Keywords: patience, waiting, surrender, sacrifice, wisdom, foresight, planning, strategy, eventual gain

The card of the Hanged Man depicts a man hanging upside down from a beam. His legs are crossed and he has reached an impasse. No further movement is possible for the time being. The card represents sacrifice and the willingness to face short-term losses to ensure long-term gains. The Fool must learn patience and how to act strategically to achieve the result he wants. An immediate advantage must be given up, but will eventually be replaced by a much better opportunity. All expectations should be surrendered for the time being.

13 Death

'I am the change that all must face in order to be born anew…'

Keywords: endings, loss, mourning, acceptance, adjustment, change, transition, rebirth, renewal

In the Rider-Waite-Smith deck, the card of Death is represented by a skeleton in armour riding a white horse over the corpse of a king. This suggests that the old order has ended and a new era is about to begin. At this stage in the journey, the Fool must accept approaching endings and uncertainty about the future. The endings may be difficult and painful, but we must learn to accept them. After a period of mourning and adjustment, we will be able to move on and embark on a new path. Change is inevitable. As we come to terms with loss, we are transformed.

14 Temperance
'I am the key to keeping your head...'

Keywords: balanced temperament, harmony, moderation, cooperation, compromise, adaptability, relationship

The Temperance card shows the figure of an angel pouring liquid from one vessel into another. This indicates that feelings are able to flow freely. It may signify a guardian angel watching over us. The card represents balance, healing and harmony. The Fool has learnt to master his thoughts and feelings and can now have harmonious relationships with others. We should act in moderation; compromise is the key to any problem. We have the ability to manage a situation and resolve problems. Events will run smoothly and success can be achieved. This card indicates that good relationships are possible.

15 The Devil
'I am the shadow you need to see the light...'

Keywords: lust, greed, rage, primal instincts, secrets, the shadow, success in career and personal interests

The Devil card may fill us with fear and dread because the Devil is a Christian symbol associated with evil. The card does not indicate evil, but asks us to confront the shadowy, instinctual part of ourselves. Following the perfect balance of the angel in the Temperance card, the Fool is reminded of those parts of himself that are self-serving and uncooperative, which he had tried to keep hidden away even from himself. When this card appears in a spread, things that we don't like to admit about our own character and desires may be trying to break into our consciousness. We may encounter these unwelcome qualities in others or in our dreams. A neglected part of us needs to be heard. Personal gain and success in one's career is indicated by this card. We are advised to act in our own interests.

16 The Tower

'I am the crises that is the making of you...'

Keywords: conflict, overthrow, disruption, disapproval, unexpected change

The Tower card shows a tall building that has been struck by lightning. It is in flames and about to topple over. The lightning signifies that the gods are angry or disapproving. The Fool encounters sudden and disruptive changes and crises which force him to question his journey. This card suggests that the times are volatile, things are not going according to plan and the old order is in danger of being overthrown. We should not try to hold on and save the toppling tower; it is better to stand back and wait for things to settle. We may face uncertainty for a while. This card asks us to re-evaluate our current path. A sudden, complete change may be the best way forward.

17 The Star

'I am hope, bright as Sirius in the night sky...'

Keywords: hope, faith, meaning, inspiration, promise, healing, protection, new horizon

The Star is a welcome symbol of hope, inspiration and rebirth to the Fool in the wake of the difficulties and uncertainties encountered in the Devil and Tower cards.

In this card we see a star shining brightly in the sky above a beautiful woman who is emptying jugs of water into a stream. It represents feelings being returned to their source. Healing is possible and our sense of well-being is renewed. There is hope for the future and new possibilities are beginning to form. We are ready to give and receive love. The Star promises change for the better. This is a good time to meet new people, apply for jobs and aspire towards what is really important to us.

18 The Moon

'I am the fear that lurks at the bottom of the water...'

Keywords: intuition, imagination, dreams, unconscious, fears, confusion, deception, disillusionment

The Moon is associated with night, the unconscious realm and the dream world, where our deepest fears and imaginations run wild. The Fool has encountered a period of confusion and disillusionment. Where is the promise of the previous card and what does the journey hold next? Situations are vague and unclear; matters are not what they seem. We can act without being seen! We are advised to avoid deception and paranoia. At this time we can more easily tap into our unconscious and find creative solutions to problems. The way ahead is foggy, but we should allow our intuition to guide us.

19 The Sun

'I am light and warmth and all good things to all people...'

Keywords: joy, optimism, clarity, trust, courage, ambition, success, opportunity, health, vitality, happiness

The Sun, shown shining on a child riding a white horse, is symbolic of life in full bloom. The Fool has passed through his dark night and the way ahead is clear again. He knows where he is going and what he wants to achieve and he meets with success in all his endeavours. Indicating energy, joy, optimism and worldly success, this card suggests that it is the perfect moment to embrace opportunities and live life to the full. When this card appears in a spread, it promises health, happiness and perhaps even the birth of a baby.

20 Judgement

'I am the one who judges the worth of the one who comes before me...'

Keywords: reward for past effort, re-evaluation, responsibility, outcome, resolution, acceptance

The Judgement card shows an angel, possibly Gabriel, sounding a trumpet above figures rising from their graves. It echoes the Day of Judgement referred to in the Bible, when Christ and his angels will return to Earth and even the dead will be judged on their deeds. This card can be understood to bring us the reward in life that we deserve. The Fool is forced to look at where he has come from, how he has behaved and the choices he has made. It marks a point at which we must re-evaluate our lives. We may need to learn hard lessons and be held responsible for past actions. We are advised to come to a resolution and move on with a clean slate. The card can also refer to judgements in law.

21 The World

'I complete the cycle that it may turn again and begin anew...'

Keywords: integration, fulfillment, achievement, completion, ending, final reward, success

The World, represented by a dancing woman, is the final card in one complete cycle. The creatures at each corner of this card signify the four elements – fire (lion), earth (bull), air (eagle) and water (merman) – that form the fabric of our world. The Fool has accomplished much and learnt what he is capable of along the way. Challenges have been faced and battles fought and won.

He is now ready to resume his position at the start of a new cycle. New challenges beckon and they can be approached with confidence. All things will be possible in the fullness of time.

THE MINOR ARCANA – day-to-day life, people and experiences

Wands

Wands are associated with the element of fire and represent sparks of energy and the life force. They are represented by branches which are sprouting leaves, suggesting creation, regeneration and potential for the future. There is a great deal of energetic activity in the wands, which translates into action – sometimes creative and sometimes defensive or aggressive. Many wands in a spread indicate that events are moving quickly. Wands are sometimes referred to by other names, including rods, staves, staffs and batons, depending on which deck of cards or book you use.

Ace of Wands

Keywords: beginning, change, opportunity, adventure, creativity, hope, action

The Ace of Wands signifies new beginnings and opportunities that can mark a change of direction in a person's life. There is the chance to embark on a journey or adventure, which may be sparked off by a new job opportunity, enterprise or relationship. The situation is full of hope and creative potential. It can also presage a birth in the family. Follow your intuition in taking up the right opportunities. Decide what you want to do and act quickly or you may miss your chance.

Two of Wands

Keywords: rest after hard work, patience, trust, planning for the future

The Two of Wands indicates that a new goal or project is on the horizon. It has taken courage, care and determination to formulate your plan, so now you can stand back and allow it to unfold and grow. Leaving the matter alone to allow the magic to work can lead to a period of restlessness. Patience and trust in the future are required. At this time you should make plans for the next stage and work out what to do once your creative endeavours have taken root and started to grow. Negotiations with others may be required. Travel may be indicated.

Three of Wands

Keywords: accomplishment, success, satisfaction, progression

The Three of Wands represents hopes and plans that have been realized in the world. As the image on the card suggests, your ships are sailing home and success is on the horizon. The first stage of a project has been completed and there is a feeling of great satisfaction and pride in your accomplishment. But remember there is much work ahead so you must not become complacent. Avoid arrogance and remember you have not always been this fortunate and could lose your fortune again. The momentum of your success may propel you into the next stage of your project or creative endeavour.

Four of Wands

Keywords: reward, blessing, celebration, happiness, harmony, romance

The Four of Wands suggests that you can reap the rewards of your achievements. The card promises a time of peace and harmony. It is a temporary calm before the storm – more hard work and energy will be required again soon to resolve problems and conflicts that will arise. But for the time being a great deal of satisfaction and celebration is in order.

Be charming and amiable and enjoy sharing your success with others. Romance may be in the air.

Five of Wands

Keywords: fighting, conflict, obstacles, compromise

The fives of each suit mark the crunch points along the journey. The Five of Wands suggests conflict, as demonstrated by the fight scene on the card. It can also indicate the possibility of lawsuits. In your effort to accomplish your goals you have had to make difficult decisions and possibly cut corners or stepped on other people's toes along the way. This may have been unavoidable, but now you must battle it out. Try not to compete, but find a way to resolve the matter; compromise, if necessary. You need to hammer out the problem and find a resolution. If you behave honourably, things could turn out to your advantage.

Six of Wands

Keywords: success, leadership, resolution, fortune, acclaim

In the Six of Wands, problems have been dealt with and a matter is on the point of being successfully resolved. You have the support of friends and colleagues in realising your aims. Good news is on the way, so don't give up now. You should stay true to your original vision and goals. The card may indicate that you will receive public acclaim for your activities and efforts. Exams will have a positive outcome. Relationships are about to take a turn for the better.

Seven of Wands

Keywords: upper hand, position of advantage, challenge, force, reassessment

With the Seven of Wands you face another battle with others, but this time you have the upper hand.

Remember to play fair, but maintain control over a situation and keep applying force. In the process you will learn to harness your competitive instincts to defend yourself and your creative endeavours. The challenges you face can also help you to reassess your plans and goals and modify your behaviour as required. This will make you stronger and more successful in the long run.

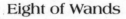

Eight of Wands

Keywords: movement, progress, back on track, goals on their way to being achieved

The Eight of Wands represents a plan on its way to completion. You are back on track after a period of conflict and delay. Obstacles have been cleared and the way is free. You are focused on attaining your goals and forging ahead with your plans. Things are on the move. News may herald major changes in your life. Events are moving quickly and circumstances will soon change for the better. Things you hoped for will come to pass. Travel may be required to secure a matter in your favour.

Nine of Wands

Keywords: final challenge, goal in sight, perseverance, tenacity, determination, courage to overcome

The Nine of Wands represents last-minute challenges on your way to attaining a goal. You have come a long way and are determined not to give up now. Although it may not seem like it at the moment, what you have been hoping for is within reach. With your goal in sight, you find the courage and tenacity to give one final push. If you persevere, no obstacle can stand in your way for long. From deep within you must find the resources to keep going and remain hopeful. You have been given a final chance to prove you are worthy of success, it is up to you to rise to the challenge.

Ten of Wands

Keywords: achievement, attainment of goals, satisfaction, experience gained, rest and regeneration needed

In the Rider-Waite-Smith deck, the Ten of Wands shows an old man reaching his final destination. He is hunched over with the weight of his load. You have come a long way and are weighed down with the responsibility of turning your vision into reality. Your efforts are about to pay off, but at a cost for you have been shaped by bitter experience and have lost the innocence and optimism of youth. As you reach the end of the cycle you can find satisfaction in all your achievements so far. You will need to rest and recharge your batteries so that new ideas can form and you can start the process again.

Page of Wands

Keywords: active, playful, imaginative, inspired, creative, youthful, folly

The Page of Wands is an active and boisterous youth with a fertile imagination. This card represents the urge to explore and play, to follow your dreams and look for new experiences and adventures. The Page seeks to avoid the responsibility that comes with maturity. When this card appears, it may represent a person, young or old, whose behaviour is eternally youthful. It may also represent your own need to break from stifling habits and responsibilities and develop these creative qualities within yourself.

Knight of Wands

Keywords: honourable, courageous, hasty, unreliable, aggressive, volatile, new direction

The Knight of Wands is a great warrior who loves to take risks and prove himself worthy. An honourable opponent, he defends the vulnerable and fights for their cause. He can be hot-headed and temperamental and may rush to conclusions. The card may describe someone you know who fits these characteristics or could indicate that you need to develop your warrior-like qualities to defend yourself or your loved ones. The Knight of Wands often signifies a move to a new home or a new direction in life.

Queen of Wands

Keywords: strong, courageous, generous, vibrant, creative, wise, intuitive

The Queen of Wands is a wise woman, independent and authoritative, imaginative and intuitive, strong and courageous. She knows what she wants and how to get it. The Queen makes a warm, lively host who is generous with her gifts. The card may describe a woman you know who fits these characteristics or may indicate that you need to develop these qualities yourself.

King of Wands

Keywords: intuitive, decisive, active, inspirational, visionary

The King of Wands is a mature man of vision who inspires others. He has strong leadership qualities and uses his wisdom and powers of intuition to guide him in decision-making. Sprightly and full of energy, the King engages with life to the full. The card could describe a man you know who fits these characteristics or indicate that you need to develop these qualities of leadership, activity and inspiration.

Cups

Cups are associated with the element of water and represent feelings, love, relationships and emotional fulfilment. They also signify the vast imaginative reserves within us and our unconscious realm.

Water quenches our thirst and brings satisfaction and fulfilment. The cups themselves are vessels for holding water and they are often full (indicating fulfilment); however, sometimes the water is spilt (indicating crisis and sorrow) or overflowing (suggesting abundance). Many cups in a spread signify that feelings and relationships are highlighted. The cups are sometimes referred to by other names, including chalices, goblets and cauldrons, depending on which deck of cards or book you use.

Ace of Cups

Keywords: love, joy, happiness, abundance, relationship, emotional expression, fertility

The Ace of Cups, like the overflowing waters pictured on the card, indicates freely flowing emotions which need to find expression. There is potential for great emotional fulfilment. Deeply satisfying love and happiness are possible. The Ace of Cups represents the start of a new relationship or it can indicate a marriage proposal. There is the chance of a fresh start and a new lease of life. There is great hope for the future – your emotions will sustain you and love will find a way!

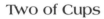

Two of Cups

Keywords: new relationship, attraction, romance, harmony, satisfaction, conception, emotional fulfilment

The Two of Cups heralds the start of a new relationship, romantic attraction or connection with another person. You have the capacity for deep satisfaction and fulfilment. It feels as though you have met your match in another person. You see yourself reflected and mirrored back by your partner and find out about new aspects of your character through his or her eyes. Existing relationships are strengthened. The card can indicate a marriage union or conception of a child or another creative endeavour.

Three of Cups

Keywords: pleasure, joy, marriage, birth, feasting, merriment, celebration, abundance, fortune

The Three of Cups indicates that there will be a happy gathering of people. This card may herald a pregnancy or marriage proposal or success in a creative endeavour close to your heart. You can be proud of your achievements. Joy and cause for celebration are indicated. This is a time to share your good fortune with others. You have renewed faith in the power of love.

Four of Cups

Keywords: dissatisfaction, boredom, discontent, depression, crisis, re-evaluation, self-questioning

In the image on the Four of Cups card a young man ignores the three cups he already has and the one being offered to him. For some reason you feel unhappy and discontented with your lot. You are in danger of developing a careless attitude towards life and becoming apathetic. You are entering a period of personal crisis and questioning and you have temporarily lost your connection with loved ones. You may feel that something is lost or missing from your life. The card indicates that you don't realise how fortunate you are. You need to take time to re-evaluate your life and decide what is really important to you.

Five of Cups

Keywords: loss, sorrow, regret, despair, betrayal, neglect, emotional breakdown, relationship breakup

The Five of Cups can presage a relationship or marriage breakup. The image on the card shows a man in a black cloak turning his back and withdrawing from the world. Three cups have been spilled on the ground, indicating relationships that have been lost or thrown away. However, two full cups remain: this means you have a chance to hold on to whatever is left. You should think carefully before coming to a decision, for the effect could have consequences for yourself and your loved ones.

Six of Cups

Keywords: calm, serenity, acceptance, simple pleasures, nostalgia, old friends, new hope and opportunity

The Six of Cups is the calm after an emotional storm. Although things might not be perfect, you learn to accept your limits and find a new appreciation of those close to you and with whom you share your life. Your thoughts may be focused on the past and you may start to idealise the 'good times' as you remember them. An old friend may re-enter your life and help you come to terms with what you have become, bringing a fresh opportunity and a new lease of life. New friendships can also blossom. Hope in the future will be renewed.

Seven of Cups

Keywords: decision, choice, dream, vision, imagination, new path

The Seven of Cups suggests you are at a crossroads in life or in a particular matter. You have a very important decision to make and there appears to be more than one option open to you. In this card you see the cups situated in rows in the clouds. Each cup is filled with a different magical item. You may rely on the imagination, a dream or a vision to choose the right path. But you are advised to remain grounded and realistic when working with the imaginary realm or your decisions will be short-lived and you won't be able to stick with them for long.

Eight of Cups

Keywords: retreat, escape, abandonment, loss, dissatisfaction, time out, perspective needed

The Eight of Cups indicates that you may need to go away for a while to work out what is really important to you. You are unfulfilled and dissatisfied with your choices and find it difficult to choose something and stick with it. Nothing seems to bring the satisfaction for which you are yearning. You must find a way to gain some perspective on your life before deciding what to do next. The card can indicate that the time has come to move on. You may need to find a way to let something go and trust that things are on the right track. You may also need to lose something for a while before it comes back.

Nine of Cups

Keywords: wishes fulfilled, hopes realised, positive outcome, childbirth, joy, success, reward

The Nine of Cups is known as the 'nine months card' and indicates the birth of a baby or another creative endeavour. Something you have tended and nurtured has come to fruition. You are brimming with joy and the world is filled with hope again. Health and happiness are offered and the problems of the past have evaporated. A wish will be fulfilled and things will work out unexpectedly well. You can enjoy your good fortune and find satisfaction in what you have achieved.

Ten of Cups

Keywords: lasting happiness, joy, fulfilment, emotional stability, fortunate outcome

The Ten of Cups is a card of emotional security and long-lasting fortune in matters of the heart. More happiness than you might have thought possible will be yours. The card indicates you have met, or will meet, the person with whom you want to spend the rest of your life. A situation has the best possible outcome. A stable, lasting relationship and family life are indicated. You can relax and enjoy the rewards of your efforts and good fortune.

The Page of Cups

Keywords: sensitive, sympathetic, kind, imaginative, poetic, lazy, daydreamer

The Page of Cups is a sensitive youth – a kind, generous soul who is easily hurt, feels other people's pain and is sympathetic to their needs. The Page may be naturally lazy at times and prone to daydreaming. He needs plenty of space to play and explore the imaginative realm. He or she may be oversensitive and may not take criticism well. News from a loved one could be indicated. This card may suggest a character who displays these qualities, or infer that these characteristics need to be developed within ourselves.

The Knight of Cups

Keywords: romantic, chivalrous, idealistic, questing, highly principled, on a mission

The Knight of Cups is the knight in shining armour of the pack, in all his romantic splendour. He rides around the kingdom searching for his love, ready to save her from any misfortune and ride off with her into the sunset. The Knight may also be on another quest – to seek the Holy Grail and restore the health of the King, bringing balance, peace and harmony to the kingdom. This card may describe a chivalrous young man or woman with a sense of mission and high ideals or it may highlight these characteristics within ourselves.

The Queen of Cups

Keywords: emotional, sensitive, caring, peace-loving, harmonious, imaginative, creative talents

The Queen of Cups is in touch with her feelings. Wise and peace-loving, she is in tune with others. She is sensitive, sympathetic and kind-hearted. A good listener, she can advise others on matters that are causing concern. The Queen is a highly imaginative woman with creative gifts and talents. This card can represent a mature woman with these characteristics or it can refer to these qualities in your own character.

The King of Cups

Keywords: kind, honourable, responsible, respected, considerate, easily swayed

The King of Cups is a kind, honourable male who is trusted and respected by others. He is naturally caring and puts the needs of his subjects first.

A just and fair ruler, he has earned the respect of others. He can be easily swayed and manipulated, however, so may become distrustful of others' motives. This card can be chosen to represent an individual with these qualities, or it may highlight these tendencies within ourselves.

Swords

Swords are associated with the element of air and represent ideas, rational thought and communication. They concern the ideals of truth and justice. The swords are active principles and the cards describe circumstances in which you are called to fight for what you believe in. Their blades are notoriously double-edged, indicating that every decision you make or ideal you support may have both beneficial and harmful consequences. Swords are made of cold, hard metal, suggesting a lack of feeling or emotion. A number of swords in a spread indicates a focus on thinking – you may be called to fight for or be forced to reconsider your beliefs and ideals. Swords are sometimes referred to by other names, including daggers, knives and blades, depending on which deck of cards or book you use.

Ace of Swords

Keywords: beginning, hope, ideals, principles, justice, conquest, new direction

The Ace of Swords stands for your principles and ideals. You have decided to embark on a new life or take a new direction and have high expectations of your future. Justice will be done. You do not wish to compromise your strongly held beliefs. The card may indicate the birth of a child, bringing great hope for the future. You are asked to have faith in yourself and your ability to overcome any challenges that lie ahead.

Two of Swords

Keywords: tension, balance, stalemate, difficult decision, action needed

The Two of Swords indicates that a matter is in the balance and a difficult decision must be made. You cannot decide between two options open to you. The figure in the image on the card is blindfolded, suggesting that the way ahead is obscured. You must make a decision and stick by it. You should act now and not allow fears and doubts to hold you back. The sooner you make a decision, the sooner you can move on and find relief from a situation that is hanging over you.

Three of Swords

Keywords: conflict, struggle, heartache, disappointment, arguments, tears, separation

The Three of Swords has the stark image of a heart with three swords passed through it. This card suggests the experience of pain and disappointment in matters of the heart, perhaps because of a love triangle. Feelings may be sacrificed in the interest of rational thinking. Quarrels and squabbles with loved ones are indicated. A separation of some kind may result. In gaining some distance from the matter you will find relief and realise that change was necessary in the long run.

Four of Swords

Keywords: rest, retreat, withdrawal, recuperation, relief from anxieties, rebuilding strength

The Four of Swords offers solace from a matter that has caused anguish. The card shows the tomb of a knight in a church; the effigy has his hands clasped in prayer. Something has been lost and part of you feels as though it has died with it. You need time alone to contemplate what has happened and where things might have gone wrong. You must rebuild your strength and reorganise your thoughts before you are ready to face the world again.

Five of Swords

Keywords: unfair play, dishonour, belligerence, loss, facing consequences

The Five of Swords indicates unfair play and belligerent actions without consideration of their effects in the long run. You may have the upper hand in a matter, but your victory is double-edged and causes as much sorrow to you as it does to your adversaries. You have acted dishonourably and disobeyed authority to gain the upper hand. You must swallow your pride and approach a situation honestly and be prepared to face the consequences of your actions.

Six of Swords

Keywords: solace, respite, retreat, healing, journey, insight, reputation restored

The Six of Swords may suggest that every ounce of strength has been sapped from you following a tough time, but the worst has now passed. The card indicates that a journey might be the best way to resolve a matter; this may be a journey in the literal sense or a journey of the mind. You are confronted with your subconscious thoughts and, as a result, insights may arise. You should allow things to sort themselves out without intervening. A matter that has been causing you great concern is on its way to being resolved.

Seven of Swords

Keywords: cunning, guile, deceit, tact, diplomacy, flexibility, compromise for the greater good

The Seven of Swords indicates that a situation calls for you to behave falsely in order to attain positive results. The card shows a figure stealing swords from a military camp. While such an act may be dishonourable and your personal principles may be compromised, your actions may be necessary for the greater good. This card suggests there are times when your beliefs and ideals must be flexible and you should adapt them to the task at hand. Life throws many situations at us and we can't afford to be too rigid in our thinking when we come to deal with them.

Eight of Swords

Keywords: restriction, mistrust, inability to act, indecision, imprisonment, isolation from others

The Eight of Swords represents restriction and mistrust. Like the Two of Swords, the figure in this card is blindfolded and afraid to act and face the consequences. But the figure on the Eight of Swords is bound and surrounded by a wall of swords, as if held in a prison. A situation seems hopeless and you can't see a way out. You have run out of excuses and of ways to avoid making a decision – there is no escape. You must learn to trust others and should not be afraid to ask for help. You need to rebuild your connection with others and end your isolation before a decision is possible.

Nine of Swords

Keywords: fear, doubt, anxiety, nightmares, troubled conscience, suffering, despair

The Nine of Swords represents great anxiety and suffering. The figure depicted on the card is in bed but unable to sleep; she holds her head in despair. Your hopes have been dashed, you are filled with fear and doubt and you struggle to come to terms with a matter. You blame yourself for an unfortunate outcome, but need to keep things in perspective. While it is necessary to face your part in a situation, you are only human and will make mistakes. You need to forgive and accept your limitations before you can lay the past to rest and move on.

Ten of Swords

Keywords: endings, misfortune, loss, defeat, new understanding, fresh perspective

The Ten of Swords represents defeat and marks the end of a difficult matter. The image on the card is of a man lying on the ground with ten swords in his back. At the end of a long struggle, something has been irrevocably lost. You must put the past behind you and move on to the next stage of the cycle. While you have been defeated on this occasion, lessons have been learned and you will move on with a new understanding of yourself and a fresh perspective.

Page of Swords

Keywords: curiosity, intelligence, wit, honesty, independence, clash with authority

The Page of Swords is a clever, witty youth with a natural curiosity and inquisitive nature. He is in the process of developing his own ideas and beliefs and may frequently clash with authority over differences of opinion. The youth's independent ideas and curious spirit should be encouraged and nurtured rather than quashed. This card may represent a boy or girl who displays these qualities or may suggest that such gifts should be developed by the querent.

Knight of Swords

Keywords: fighter, warrior, reformer, prepared to make sacrifices for just causes

The Knight of Swords is a brave warrior who fights for the causes he believes in and is charged to protect. The Knight challenges injustice wherever he sees it and shows courage against all odds. He is willing to make sacrifices to uphold his principles and fights for justice, fairness and reform. Change will be brought about. This card may represent a young man or woman who displays these qualities or could suggest the time is right for the querent to develop such characteristics.

Queen of Swords

Keywords: just, fair, intelligent, faithful, warrior, strong beliefs, idealistic, highly principled.

The Queen of Swords has a strong mind and keen intelligence. With a cool exterior, she may sometimes seem icy or aloof, but she is always kind and fair toward her subjects. The Queen will argue her opinions with a clear head and keen insight. She is not afraid to fight for her principles if her duties require it.

When this card is selected, it may represent a female who displays these qualities or may indicate the time is right for these characteristics to be developed by the querent.

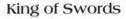

King of Swords

Keywords: intelligent, logical, fair, law-maker, judge, counsellor, warrior, strategist

The King of Swords is intelligent and known for his keen sense of logic and clear-headedness. He is an excellent judge and counsellor to his people and a capable warrior and military strategist. He has many innovative ideas, encourages reform and change and runs an orderly, civilised society. When this card is selected, it may represent a man who displays these qualities or could suggest that they should be developed by the querent.

Pentacles

Pentacles are associated with the element of earth and represent matter, the body and the physical world. Pentacles are concerned with material security and finances as well as personal values and the sense of security that comes from within. This suit also represents physical health and wellbeing and the ability to draw comfort and satisfaction from personal possessions and the physical world. The pentacles themselves are in the shape of coins, suggesting money and earnings. Another word for money is talent; the pentacles represent talents and abilities that help us earn money and contribute to society in a useful way. Many pentacles in a spread suggest that material gain is highlighted in a matter and practical action may be required. The pentacles are sometimes referred to by other names, including coins and discs, depending on which deck of cards or book you use.

Ace of Pentacles

Keywords: new venture, opportunity, promise of wealth, achievement

The Ace of Pentacles suggests a new opportunity or venture that will put our innate talents to good use. Like the other aces, this card represents high hopes for success and an opportunity to make something of our talents, provided we use them wisely.

Two of Pentacles

Keywords: balance, weighing up pros and cons, careful consideration, common sense, responsible decision-making

The Two of Pentacles is concerned with juggling or balancing two different duties, weighing up the pros and cons of a matter and making a carefully considered decision. In the image on the Rider-Waite-Smith deck, the figure balances two pentacles that are connected by the symbol of a cosmic lemiscate. This indicates that the figure must keep all his responsibilities in balance. If he fails to do so, he will be forced to drop one of the pentacles and the harmony between them will be destroyed. Behind the figure, ships sail on the ocean, but the rolling waves suggest that emotional imbalances affect your stability in the material realm. Under the circumstances, you are challenged to make the most practical choice you can.

Three of Pentacles

Keywords: craftsperson, skilled artisan, recognition of abilities, achievement

The Three of Pentacles indicates that you will be recognised for your skills and achievements. Your handiwork is appreciated by others. You have worked hard and earned your success so far. While establishing a new venture you have honed your skills and built a good reputation. Now you must reassess your goals and develop in a new direction You can start another project from a position of strength. Financial affairs will blossom.

Four of Pentacles

Keywords: thrift, over-protectiveness, lack of generosity, mistrust, paranoia, isolation

The Four of Pentacles represents a withholding, ungenerous nature. You are afraid of losing what you have gained, so you hold on tightly to everything to prevent it being snatched away. You begin to become paranoid about other people's motives and are so afraid of losing what you have that you lose touch with others and become unapproachable. This card can indicate a tendency toward obsessive compulsive behaviour, hypochondria and a fear of taking risks. It warns that self-imposed isolation and the desire for total control mean you are detached from the wider world and in danger of pushing away those who love you.

Five of Pentacles

Keywords: financial worries, fear of loss, destitution, failure, shame, re-evaluation, starting again

The Five of Pentacles indicates financial worries and fear of loss or failure. The image on the card shows two destitute figures outside a church, suggesting both material and spiritual impoverishment. The card may presage the failure of a venture, loss of a job or redundancy. You feel you have not lived up to your high standards and expectations. Your fear of loss may have led to this situation. You must reassess your behaviour and regain faith in your talents and abilities. You have the capacity to work hard, rebuild your reputation and achieve your ambitions.

Six of Pentacles

Keywords: success, sharing of wealth, charity, philanthropy, giving back to society

The Six of Pentacles signifies the sharing of good fortune with others. You have learned the lesson of the previous cards and now understand the consequence of holding on to too tightly to material possessions. Plans are working out, you have succeeded in rebuilding your reputation in the world and can celebrate your success with others. Much satisfaction is gained from sharing time and money with worthy causes.

Seven of Pentacles

Keywords: rest after work, disappointing returns, re-evaluation of projects, redirecting efforts

The Seven of Pentacles indicates weariness after a period of hard work and suggests pausing to assess what you have achieved so far. It asks you to re-evaluate your plans and take stock of a situation. Are you on the best route to success? Perhaps you are overworked and disappointed with the rewards of your labours. A period of recuperation and regeneration may be necessary and you might want to take a short break if you can afford it. You should not lose faith, but pick yourself up again and implement the improvements that are needed.

Eight of Pentacles

Keywords: new skills, apprenticeship, confidence, job satisfaction, reward

The Eight of Pentacles represents learning a new skill. You may be training in a new trade fairly late in life. You are slowly but surely gaining mastery in your work and can reap the rewards of your efforts so far. Financial gain and job satisfaction are indicated. Faith in your skills and confidence that you will achieve your ambitions will help you stay on the right path.

Nine of Pentacles

Keywords: pleasure, self-esteem, humility, realistic evaluation, sense of achievement, satisfaction, windfall

The Nine of Pentacles indicates that you can take pleasure and satisfaction in your work and reap the rewards of your labours. You have worked hard to develop your talents and abilities and have proved yourself a capable and worthy member of society. You are realistic about your limitations and recognise that you have had failures along the way. However, you can be proud of everything you have achieved so far and can draw great satisfaction from recognising where you have come from and what you have been through to get where you are today. An inheritance or unexpected windfall might be indicated by this card.

Ten of Pentacles

Keywords: security, inheritance, lasting success, satisfaction, sharing, rewards, contentment

The Ten of Pentacles indicates that lasting success and material satisfaction have been achieved. You have earned the right to relax and enjoy what has been accumulated through your efforts. The card suggests that you have also gained an inner sense of security. In addition to your personal wealth, a family inheritance may ensure that you live in comfort for a long time. Enjoying the company of your family and loved ones and sharing your material fortune with them brings the greatest pleasure now. The card indicates a satisfying home life and the chance to pass on a positive inheritance to your descendants.

Page of Pentacles

Keywords: diligent, reliable, mature, loyal, steady, hardworking, responsible

The Page of Pentacles is mature beyond his years and is the type of youth you can depend on – reliable and hard working in his studies and keen to start working from an early age. The Page of Pentacles makes a loyal, steady friend. A message about money may be received. The Page may represent a youthful person who displays these qualities or may highlight the need to nurture these qualities in ourselves.

Knight of Pentacles

Keywords: sensible, considerate, stable, responsible, respectful, practical, nervous

The Knight of Pentacles is a practical, sensible, considerate character, with a strong sense of duty and respect for others. Unlike the other knights, the Knight of Pentacles acts with caution, taking care not to rock the boat. Knights are normally very active principles who fight for change of some sort. This knight needs to find a way of balancing these two tendencies or they will pull in different directions and lead to nervous tension. This card may represent a young man or woman known for these qualities, or may indicate the need to develop them in our own characters.

Queen of Pentacles

Keywords: generous stable, sensible, down-to-earth, warm, comforting, healthy, contented

The Queen of Pentacles is practical, down-to-earth and generous with her gifts. She has an affinity with nature and animals and radiates comfort and confidence in her body. She enjoys tending to her surroundings and taking care of others. She can be relied upon to give fair, sensible advice and find practical solutions to problems. This card may represent a mature woman who displays these qualities or can highlight the need to develop them in ourselves.

King of Pentacles

Keywords: sensible, fair, honest, patient, generous, practical, traditional, stable, humble, self-reliant

The King of Pentacles is an honest, generous leader who has worked hard and achieved great success. He upholds his duties and traditions and respects his ancestral heritage. The King finds practical solutions to problems and dislikes experimenting with new methods and technologies, preferring the old way of doing things. The King is kind, but has high expectations of others and expects them to have the same self-discipline and work ethic that he has. He is humble and self-reliant. This card can represent a mature man who displays these qualities or can indicate the need to recognise them in ourselves.

Divination with Playing Cards

'Ordinary' playing cards are derived from the Minor Arcana and court cards of the Tarot. The first cards to arrive in Britain came from France five hundred years ago, probably from the city of Rouen, and the design of the cards is still based on a pattern used all those years ago. The court cards still show figures wearing clothes that date back to the fourteenth century. According to legend these costumes derive from the pack designed by Odette, the mistress of Charles VI of France, having been given a pack by travellers who brought them from the East.

The suitmarks – spades, hearts, diamonds and clubs – are also French, although we have given them English names. Since they were introduced to Britain, what we now call 'the English pattern' has spread to the United States and other English-speaking countries. In other parts of the world, playing cards have developed differently. France uses cards that are slightly different from ours, although the four suits remain the same; Italy, Spain, Germany and Switzerland have packs that are all quite different. Clubs becomes Acorns in Germany and Switzerland and Swords in Italy and Spain. Diamonds are Bells in Germany and Switzerland and Coins in Italy and Spain. Spades are Flowers in Switzerland, Leaves in Germany and Batons in Spain and Italy. And Hearts are Shields in the Swiss pack, Hearts in the German one and Cups in the other two.

What is constant is that in these, and in all other countries where cards are played, they are used to divine the future – and, being descended from the Tarot, probably always have been. The same legend that credits Odette with designing the court cards also has it that she and her royal lover were shown the oracular power of the cards by a fortune-teller who not only correctly foretold events but also whispered secrets that were only known to the King and his paramour. Another charming legend has it that Napoleon used the power of the pack to divine the right moment to mount his campaign to win the heart of Josephine Beauharnais. We don't know what spread he used, but we do know he captured her affections and held them until politics demanded that he divorce her in favour of an Austrian princess.

As with the Tarot, the cards may be read for you or for anyone else and can be used to answer a simple question or to give a more in-depth reading.

Tradition has it that cards that are to be used for divinatory purposes should be used for no other purpose and should be wrapped in black silk when not in use.

Some people also believe that if the cards are kept on a high shelf, this raises what the cards say to a level that is above worldliness.

If the reading is for someone else, shuffle the pack first and then give it to the querent (some say left hand to left hand, but as usual let instinct be your guide) to be shuffled or mixed again.

The pack is now cut three times by the querent, again with the left hand, and the cards spread out face down, either in an overlapping row or a circle. (The reason for using the left hand is that it is believed to have symbolic access to the right side of the brain, the side that controls intuition.) The cards to be read are then selected at random, and put in the spread.

Any of the spreads that we looked at earlier can be used when using ordinary cards to divine the future. When reading, think about whether any one suit predominates. Or is one notable by its absence? This can be as significant as the cards themselves. An abundance of clubs for example may indicate that career matters are to the fore. Similarly, if the same card from each suit appears, this will also be significant. Four of the same number indicates a heightened result; three indicate that different forces are acting in harmony; and two of the same number can foretell conflicts of interest, reconciliation or maybe a new connection, depending on the suits.

Another method is, once the cards have been shuffled by both reader and querent, to spread the cards out, face down, into a semicircle. Ask the questioner to select thirteen cards and put the rest of the cards to one side. Take the baker's dozen, turn them over one by one and read what your instinct and experience tell you, remembering that the card preceding and the card following will probably have some sort of connection.

This done, marry the thirteen cards with the rest of the pack. From now on, only the reader must shuffle or mix the cards. Spread the cards out, face down, in a semicircle and ask the querent to select any five cards. Turn them over one by one, explaining the significance of each one, and again remembering the influence of the card before and the card that follows.

Now put these five cards back in the pack and again shuffle them well. Ask the questioner to cut the pack into three, turn up each set and read the top three cards in each one, again remembering the way in which they temper each other. Now, with all the cards face down, shuffle the pack one last time, and ask the querent to cut the pack in half. Turn each half face up – the cards that reveal themselves represent the final outcome of most of the querent's hopes and wishes, the problems they will encounter and the answers that will help them to overcome these.

The meaning of the cards

Because, in many cases, the position of the cards can change their significance, their individual and relative meanings can often be widely different. What follows can only be general. But experience shows that even so, this can be surprisingly accurate. As in most card games, the Ace is highest in value and importance.

Clubs

Clubs are linked with ambitions and achieving them successfully, with career matters, health, business partnerships, communication and expansion. The suit also has strong connections with older, mature people.

The Ace signifies a new beginning and fresh ambitions. New ideas will flow from you and could lead to a new perspective on old problems or a chance to travel. It may indicate that the questioner yearns to be free from a restrictive situation. It can also say that illness lies ahead: if followed by a heart card it will afflict someone in the immediate family.

The King combines success and ambition, innovation and communication skills. But such a man can be impatient and insensitive to the needs of others. In matters of principle he is uncompromising. His appearance often presages that a dark, friendly man will lend a helping hand just when it is most needed.

The Queen is dark, gentle and pleasing. A good organizer with the energy who embodies the old saying, 'If you want something done, ask a busy woman.' She is tactful and can usually get what she wants without stepping on too many toes. But she can use up her energy and become overtired. She suggests that such a person will offer help. Trust her.

The Jack rushes from one activity to another with all the energy of youth. He is sincere but impetuous, prone to giving up if things don't go well. That said, he can become over-absorbed in a project when it is going smoothly. He foretells the appearance of a dark young man who is confused about something. It will be to the querent's advantage if they try to make him feel at ease.

The Ten says that a long-term goal is about to be realized and that it may involve a change of direction and the chance to learn new skills. Whoever draws this card can look to the future confident that personal happiness is certain. It can also suggest a legacy from an unexpected source, but also the loss of a good friend's company.

The Nine reflects overwhelming responsibilities leading to self-doubt and loss of confidence. So now is the time to delegate and press on with core matters confidently and with conviction. It says that if a friend offers advice, consider it very, very carefully before acting on it. In the longer term, it suggests that widowhood will come but not until old age has arrived.

The Eight says that now is the time to grab sudden opportunities that show themselves. This could be the time to strike out on your own because you are enjoying or are about to experience an upsurge in energy. It could also be that an invitation is about to wing its way towards you: think twice before accepting it. It also warns against indulging in speculation and to beware of a greedy individual.

The Seven denotes personal success and satisfaction, but in achieving this, personal principles may have to be fought for. Happiness is on the horizon or just over it and will come with the achievement of a long-term goal. The card can also be a warning to beware of the opposite sex and that if you are asked to sign an important document, to take legal advice if you have any doubts about it.

The Six forecasts a period of calm on the work front, the perfect time to take a break and recharge your batteries. Use this time to network and establish contacts for new ventures. If you have been under the weather, you will probably have noticed that you are feeling better, something that is set to continue. If someone new is introduced into your circle, welcome them with open arms and you will make a friend for life.

The Five often turns up to tell the querent that this is the time to argue their case, especially regarding matters outside the home. Tiredness and carelessness brought about by the stress of being involved in other people's problems may cause accidents to happen and ill-health could be about to lay you low. Rivals could well be particularly uncommunicative and if you receive a letter from one, read between the lines, especially if it comes from abroad. It's not all bad news, though. The Five indicates a good and happy marriage.

The Four tells you that it's time to move on, and shake off the yokes in which others have bound you. It's also a time when you have to win the trust of others, to establish clear communication even if in doing so you feel you are holding yourself back. It may also be that a friend lets you down about a promise made earlier. Before you let fly at them, find out why: there could be a very good reason for their change of heart.

The Three says that an opportunity to expand your horizons is about to present itself. If you have been putting off making decisions about travel, make them now. On the work front, extra commitments, new opportunities and the input you are expected to put into them will require all your energy. The card can also indicate that the querent will be married more than once and news that a young person is ill may be received. But it is not too serious.

The Two indicates a disappointment of some sort, but don't give in to the temptation to bottle things up. This could be the time to reflect on things, and it may herald a period when plans that involve others appear to be restrictive.

The card also advises that the questioner needs to work to achieve a balance between work and health, and that, to succeed, a business relationship may have to be reassessed.

Diamonds

Diamonds refer to practical matters – money, property in general and the home, animals and children. The suit reflects qualities of patience.

The Ace augurs new ventures of a practical or financial nature. It promises a flood of prosperity and perhaps a change of home. But the surge in prosperity that is in the air lessens if the card is followed by a spade.

The King is a reliable man on whom you can always depend and turn to for advice, the sort of person who ensures that your life runs as smoothly as possible. He is patient and affectionate, but when he does show this side of his character, he does so in deeds rather than words. The King promises a great deal of travel.

The Queen is a practical and organized woman, one often in a long-term relationship. She is good at solving problems, particularly other people's. She has the happy talent of making everyone feel at home. Get her on your side and she will stick by you through thick and thin. But every coin has two sides, and if the Queen appears hard-hearted she is not to be trusted.

The Jack is a practical person who has youth on his side. He always shows common sense and a helpful attitude to others. These attributes and the responsible way he handles money might make him seem wise beyond his years. Like the Queen he is supportive in good times and bad.

The Ten radiates success, either financial or domestic. But if money is about to change hands, make sure that you are in control of the situation. The card smiles upon new plans, including a new domestic commitment, which it ensures will be successful.

The Nine counsels independent thought and action. It recommends putting personal interests first and says that the way to success is through expanding the horizons and perhaps speculating a little. A new business will bloom, but there may be a deal of extra work involved in making sure that it is firmly rooted.

The Eight announces the discovery of a new skill, which might well boost the income. It also says that there may be an unexpected change in domestic and financial arrangements. Any restless feelings experienced now should be channelled into making tangible improvements to your life. A short journey with some sort of bonus at the end can also be presaged by this card.

The Seven brings harmony at home and to financial matters. It favours long-term plans and says, 'don't rely on common sense all the time; trust your intuition and trust your dreams'. New happiness could well come into your life courtesy of children or maybe animals. There's also the whiff of change in the air, perhaps in the form of a new job.

The Six stresses that if you receive any documents, remember that the Devil is in the detail. Avoid making too many commitments now and keep a cautious watch on your finances, for this is a time for conserving energies and reflecting on things rather than rushing into action. And if anything is going to take up more time than usual, it will be family matters. An unexpected gift could also be coming your way.

The Five may put temporary financial or practical obstacles in your path and these may make you feel isolated or detached from life. But don't give up, look for advice or a new source of help, and whatever you do don't abandon plans: modify them, building on them to move on to greater things. Be on guard lest you lose something of value when this card turns up, especially if it is followed by a spade card.

The Four puts limits on monetary and practical matters and makes you ask whether you should keep what you have, or take a chance with it. There may be difficult decisions to be made concerning the home or the family, especially children. And even if the problems you face concerning property and money seem insoluble, hang on in there: they're not. If you are approached by someone, especially a fair young man, and asked for a loan a day or two after this card appears, make sure that you know exactly what is involved.

The Three suggests that a recently embarked-on venture is built on solid foundations. It can also presage a birth in the family (the chances of this are increased many fold if the Ace turns up in the same spread). Extra commitments or responsibilities may seem something of a burden, but they will be worth it in the long term. A disappointment regarding a journey may be in the offing, especially if the card is followed by a club.

The Two says that a new venture will turn out to be built on firm foundations. Increased prosperity is on the cards, too, as well as the prospect of a change of address.

Hearts

This suit is linked with love and emotions, relationships and intuitions, young people who have left their teenage years behind but have not reached forty and people, regardless of age, who are in love.

The Ace signifies that the querent is on the brink of a new friendship that could blossom into romance. It also says that while one chapter in the book in which the emotions are written may be about to close, the first words have been written in a new one, especially if a romance has just come to an end. If a sudden burst of intuition has just been or is experienced in the near future, trust it.

The King indicates a charismatic, older man who has the happy knack of making people he talks to feel that they are the only people in the whole world who really matter. When he is faithful, he is a tender-hearted romantic, but he can wear his heart on his sleeve, so beware. The King can also represent an altruistic type who, in accepting the burden for his share of the world's troubles, puts his personal emotions on the sidelines.

The Queen is an older woman who is established in a long-term relationship. She is a caring, nurturing person who is always willing to lend an ear to those with troubles to share. And therein lies her weakness. She has a tendency to sentimentality and is prone to letting herself be so flooded by the sorrows and emotional needs of others that she drowns her own identity. And her willingness to be the emotional blotting paper of others may mean that they never reach full emotional independence.

The Jack is the one who, more than any other, loves being in love – but for sentiment's sake. The card indicates a young person, or an older, emotionally vulnerable, incurable romantic who is seeking perfection. He can also stand for the querent's best friend.

The Ten indicates that when emotional happiness and fulfilment come it will be through others. It is a lovely card to turn up, indicating someone who gives emotionally with every ounce of their being and who gets tremendous satisfaction from caring. It is a card of happy marriage blessed with many children and long-term, permanent relationships. The ten of hearts alters the negativity of any adjacent bad card and makes positive ones even more so.

The Nine, sometimes known as the card of the heart's desire or the wish card, is one of self-confidence and emotional independence. It talks of happiness in love or that a new venture of some kind will bring a rise in esteem and a boost to the finances.

The Eight warns to beware of jealousy, of emotional blackmail and says that a strong emotional attachment could be potentially destructive and should be brought to an end. But it can mean good news, signifying a holiday or break with a loved one or a friend whose company will bring great pleasure, and that one relationship is about to enter a new phase.

The Seven tells you to trust your instincts and intuition, to listen to what your dreams are saying to you. It says that you are in tune spiritually with those close to you and that friends and colleagues are in a mood of happy co-operation. Conversely, depending on the other cards in the spread, it can warn you to be on your guard lest someone you thought was a friend turns out to be fickle and false.

The Six presages a time of harmony in friendship and harmony in love. Good friends will bring a positive influence to bear on your life and if there have been rifts brought about by differences in attitude, particularly with older people, accept that differences in the way we look at life need not be a barrier to friendship. The six of hearts can also herald good news about a child's endeavours paying dividends.

The Five foretells that misunderstandings and jealousy, albeit unfounded, may be about to cloud the horizon, but that if you communicate from the heart, then they won't last for long. It says that while passion is all very well it should not rule our lives. Not only that, it counsels that it is better to see a relationship for what it is and accept it for that, rather than search for the Holy Grail. It also says that an invitation with a romantic link may make you think twice but you can accept it.

The Four is a card that gives voice to the possibility of some sort of emotional choice having to be made, especially if there are any doubts about the strength of another's commitment. It is, therefore, a card that can indicate a feeling of restlessness and dissatisfaction with the emotional side of our lives. The card often appears in a spread concerning a person with a deep love of art and music.

The Three revels in the rivalry that love or even simple friendship (is there such a thing as simple friendship?) can encourage. It can indicate an emotional tug o'war between two rivals for your affections, and that the pressure, emotional blackmail even, to which you may be subject could herald a period of stress, which could be intensified by the querent's imprudence.

The Two augurs well in the love stakes, indicating that a love match is about to be made that could lead to marriage. Friendships will deepen, long-standing quarrels mend, bridges be built and two seemingly unconnected aspects of life will come together in a totally unexpected way as long as care and attention are brought to bear.

Spades

Perhaps the most challenging of the four suits, spades are associated with older people and with ageing in general. The suit is connected to the didactic, formal and traditional, to coping with challenges, especially those that can be seen as limiting in some way and to justice.

The Ace presages that a difficult time, perhaps involving some sort of sadness, is coming to an end and that a new day dawns as new challenges open new doors. The card also predicts an appreciation of a new form of learning. There is a bad side to this card, though, for it can foretell misfortune and malice. One well-known sage believes that when the Ace of Spades is facing up, news of a birth is in the offing, and conversely when facing down, there's a death in the air.

The King is not just an authority figure, but a harsh, disapproving and pedantic perfectionist. He may have accumulated a vast store of knowledge in his journey through life, but this only serves to make him impatient of the mistakes other people make. If he has an Achilles heel, it is that rather than being seen as vulnerable, he appears only happy in his own company. His appearance may signify that a legal matter concerning a dark man may affect the querent.

The Queen, often known as the Queen of Sorrows is a critical, disapproving, mature woman – the haranguing office manager, the neighbour with the malicious tongue or the music-hall mother-in-law from hell. Afraid of being alone, she becomes possessive of her family and friends, all of whom she will defend tooth and nail, for loyalty is her cardinal virtue.

When the Queen turns up in a spread, the querent is being warned not to trust such a woman, even if appearances suggest that she should.

The Jack is young, or immature, with a hurtful tongue, which gives voice to his sarcastic wit, which those at whom it is not directed often find clever and very funny. But look below this sometimes malicious façade and you may find someone who has been hurt, which is probably the reason why he is cruel and distrustful.

The Ten – the card of disappointment – but temporary disappointment, for there are good times just around the corner. It can mean that events in some aspect of life have run their course and that a new beginning beckons, so look to the future with optimism. The ten often turns up when financial worries are to the fore, news of which may be brought by a third party.

The Nine says that no obstacle is insurmountable if it is approached with courage and determination. You may think you know a little, but you know more than you may think, so if you fear failure and rejection, there's no need. Be confident and remember that victory has to be fought for, not thought about.

The Eight indicates some form of change, but only if you can cut your ties with yesterday and view the future with confidence. Don't be afraid to give voice to your fears, for if you do you will see that the future has many more possibilities than you thought possible, thanks to new contacts and previously unexplored avenues. The eight can also herald a time when frustration will turn to anger and anger to tears.

The Seven says that if logic fails and expert opinion is against you, intuition is there to be your friend. Use it. Make the most of any advantages you have over others, even if, in doing so, there could be conflict: remember, you have right on your side.

The Six signifies unexpected help from officials, which ushers in a period of unexpected calm after an unsettling time when self-doubt may have dominated thinking and actions. The card also changes things where a relationship that has been going through a bad patch is concerned, seeing it sail into much calmer waters. But, depending on the other cards, the six of spades can also indicate that angry words with someone who is not related are threatened, and the words 'think before you speak' should be kept in mind.

The Five tells you to marshal your facts and be prepared to use them if you are to avoid the spiteful actions and dishonest dealings of others. The fact that other people may not have the same high standards as the querent should not allow disillusionment to set in and cause long-laid plans to be abandoned. But seeing these through to successful completion may mean that ambition succeeds at the cost of openness.

The Four says that any inner fears that are based on past disappointments, perhaps betrayal, may strew limitations and obstacles in the path of achieving ambitions. Life's little injustices may cut deep, but the wounds are soon healed, so move forward even though doing so means taking losses that seem unfair.

The Three advises that if reason is brought to bear, rivalry and malice can be swept to one side. It says that challenges should be accepted and obstacles will be overcome even if doing so costs time and effort. And things that appear trifling now will gain significance in the future.

The Two is a card that indicates that a choice between unappealing alternatives may have to be made. Logic is called for, especially if the choice concerns conflict between two acquaintances or perhaps two distinct aspects of life. Or it could be having to choose which of two pieces of information to believe. The card can also warn to beware lest there's an unfortunate accident, that there may be a period of separation from a loved one and that spiteful gossip may hit home.

TEA LEAF READING

Reading the tea leaves – tasseography – has a long and noble history, probably beginning not long after tea was first drunk, in China, perhaps as early as 3000BCE. According to legend, the very first tea leaves came about by accident when the leaves fell into an outdoor cooking pot of water and proved to be a refreshing brew.

True or not, what we do know for a fact is that tea-drinking spread throughout the Orient and India, from whence it, and the associated tea-leaf divination, came to Europe.

Tea was an expensive luxury in Britain (so expensive that it was kept under lock and key in tea caddies) until the nineteenth century when large quantities were imported from India and Ceylon (present-day Sri Lanka), and so tasseography was a rare skill. But the art of divination from the dregs was practised long before that. The Ancient Greeks probably studied the dregs of the wine glasses for clues to what the future held, and whenever herbal remedies were brewed to give to the sick, what remained in the cup would be peered at by a spey wife (a Scottish expression for a woman who has divinatory skills).

Everyone who reads tea leaves has their own rituals and often their own interpretations of what they see.

Some people pour the tea into a cup through a strainer and either use what is there to peer into the future, or do so in association with the leaves left in the cup after it has been drunk.

Best is a good, traditional tea, the leaves of which are separate and firm, such as Earl Grey or Darjeeling. Make the tea as you usually do – most people swirl boiling water round the pot to warm it before putting the tea in – one spoon per person and 'one for the pot' is a steadfast recipe for a good brew.

As the tea is brewing (three to four minutes is usually enough) ask whoever has questions to ask to concentrate on them. It's not cheating to ask them what it is that concerns them. Pour the tea into plain white cups and enjoy drinking it – don't rush, just sip it as usual. If you want to continue concentrating, that's fine. If you want to enjoy a chat (a euphemism for a good gossip), that's all right, too, for one of the secrets of successful tea leaf reading is relaxation.

When the moment comes it's time to get down to the business in hand. As mentioned earlier, rituals vary from person to person. One well-tried and trusted method is for the querent to take the cup in their left hand and swirl it three times widdershins for a woman (clockwise for a man). The cup is then placed rim down on the saucer to drain away any tea that remains. The reader should then take the cup in their own left hand and interpret the patterns the leaves have made. Again, as with all other methods of divination, let instinct be your guide.

It's not just the leaves that are important – the position within the cup where the shapes form also influences things. For convenience the cup is mentally divided into four quarters.

The quarter nearest the handle represents the querent.

Leaves that stick to the cup in this area are concerned with him or her, their home and those closest to them. Depending on the images, masses of leaves that stick to the cup here could suggest that the questioner is being overwhelmed by responsibility for family and close friends, or it can mean that home and personal life is particularly rich.

The side opposite the handle is concerned with strangers, acquaintances rather than friends, the workplace, travel and other matters away from home. A large concentration here suggests that these are the matters that concern the querent at the moment more than the family and the home.

To the left of the handle (from the seer's angle) is the area that stands for the past, with people moving out of the querent's ken. Unusually large areas here indicate that things unresolved in the past are having a bearing on the questioner's life. This is reinforced if there is an especially large concentration of leaves in this area, and if they are particularly dark.

The part of the cup to the reader's right is the area where leaves gathered represent upcoming events and people who are about to have an influence on the querent's life. No leaves here should not be taken as a bad omen, that there is no future: rather, that the questioner is more concerned with the present and the past than with what life holds in store.

As well as being divided into four quarters, the cup is also cut in two (metaphorically speaking) horizontally. Images close to the rim indicate the present – days and weeks – those clinging to the lower part of the cup indicate the more distant future – months and years.

According to Romany tradition a dry cup heralds good news: but if there is a trace of liquid remaining in the cup, there will be tears before the week is out. Also, according to the travelling folk, the rim of the cup equates with joy and happiness, the bottom with sorrow.

An A – Z of shapes

Different symbols often mean different things to different readers. To one well-known tasseographer, an acorn indicates a pregnancy, a nearby initial giving a clue as to who will be so blessed! To another, the same symbol near the rim of the cup foretells financial success; in the middle it is equated with good health; and at the bottom it is an indication that both health and finances are due for a boost. A third reader sees the fruit of the oak tree as a general sign of health and plenty. What follows is a general guide to some of the symbols most commonly discerned in the cup.

Aeroplanes presage an unexpected journey that might be linked with a disappointment in some way. It may also mean new projects and a rise in status.

Anchors say that a journey will come to a successful end and that if the querent is at present having a bumpy ride through life, stability will soon be restored. At the top of the cup, an anchor can indicate a boost in business; if it's in the middle a voyage that boosts prosperity is indicated; and if it's near the bottom, social success is beckoning.

Angels herald good news.

Ants suggest industry and hard work, perhaps working with others to bring a project to a happy completion.

Apples promise a rosy future in business is ahead; and as they are regarded as symbols of fertility, they also represent good health.

Arches link the querent with marriage or long-term relationships. Someone regarded as an enemy may be about to extend the hand of friendship.

Arrows usually mean bad news. If the arrow is pointing towards the querent, he or she may be in danger of an attack of some kind; pointing away, he may find himself on the offensive. BUT, there is a school of thought that sees arrows as the bearers of good news in career and financial matters.

Axes may see the questioner having to chop away unpleasant difficulties.

Babies presage new interests.

Baggage – the sort you take on holiday – can mean the obvious. But it can also signify that the questioner is carrying about unnecessary emotional baggage that should be dumped as soon as possible.

Bags are a warning that a trap may be about to ensnare the querent.

Balls say that the querent will soon be bouncing back from current difficulties. Balls can also suggest that someone involved in sport will have a significant influence, probably bringing a changeable future.

Balls and chains are a sign that current commitments may be hard to shed, but that they need to be.

Balloons suggest that troubles may float in – but they will soon drift off again.

Baskets are a sign that can carry gifts with them. If full someone in or close to the family could have some news of a happily pregnant kind to impart. An empty basket, though, can mean that the questioner is giving too much of themselves to others, leaving his own emotional larder empty.

Bears bring with them a suggestion that travel to a foreign land is on the cards. A bear can also say that a strong ally will offer protection in a time of oncoming need, and that he or she will give you the strength you require to resolve a difficult situation.

Bees buzz with the news that change of some sort is in store for family or close friends.

Bells chime that marriage is in the air.

Birds sing that good news may soon be winging its way into the querent's life. If they are flying away from the handle, a departure could be round the corner, perhaps a fledgling is about to leave the nest. If they are winging their way towards the handle, a new opportunity is on the way.

Boats are an indication that some sort of important discovery is on the horizon. A boat also signifies a visit from a friend and flags a signal that soon a safe harbour will be reached.

Books, if open, suggest that startling revelations are waiting in the next chapter of life. An open book also says that to move ahead, a secret may need to be shared. It is also a sign that legal actions could follow, but that if they do they will come to a successful outcome. A closed book means that a delay of some sort will affect plans for the future.

Boots are a sign that caution is needed, according to some with the gift. To others a boot means achievement, and that if the querent is seeking protection for some reason, it will be theirs. But if the footwear is pointing away from the handle then a dismissal of some sort is in the offing. And if they are broken, then a failure looms.

Bottles suggest that illness may lie in store, but one on its own says that the querent's life will soon be bubbling over with pleasure. A full bottle is an encouraging sign to channel energy into a new challenge. An empty one is a sign of exhaustion and that health matters may soon be a cause for concern. A half-full one? It could be half-empty! And that's the difference between an optimist and a pessimist.

Boxes, when open, say that any romantic problems afflicting the questioner will soon vanish. Closed they mean that a recent lack of determination will vanish.

Branches, if in leaf, herald a birth. If bare, then disappointment of some sort looms.

Bridges present an opportunity for success that will soon cross the querent's path.

Brooms sweep change into life, suggesting that a good clear-out (both physically and emotionally) might be no bad thing.

Buildings suggest that a change of address may be just around the corner.

Butterflies say that innocent pleasures are about to flutter through the questioner's life, offering regeneration, and encouraging a carefree attitude pays dividends.

Cages are a sign that something is holding the questioner back, but they are also a sign of encouragement in that they say that the time will soon be when shackles can be shrugged off and it is time to move ahead.

Cannons see **Guns**.

Castles denote that circumstances are about to improve, especially if the questioner harbours a desire for luxury and pampering. They can also say that outside events affecting people who are not members of the immediate family are interfering with domestic happiness.

Cats bring treachery into view when they appear in the tea leaves, something that is reinforced if the feline back is arched.

Chains are a sign that links with other people will strengthen the sense of purpose.

Cherries mean that a victory of some sort is there for the taking.

Chessmen say that a short-term project should be put to one side, and that it is time to plan for the long-term if looming troubles are to be overcome. They also indicate that people are manoeuvring themselves into position for some oncoming conflict, and that it is time for the querent to follow their example.

Cliffs warn that the querent may be about to walk into a dangerous situation. But they can also suggest that the time has come to cast convention aside and live a little dangerously.

Clouds darken the bright skies of life with all sorts of doubts, but they should clear – eventually.

Clover is always regarded as a lucky symbol in reality, and it retains its fortunate connotations in the teacup, heralding as it does, prosperity in the offing.

Coffins signify if not death, then a loss of some kind.

Coins are a sign that money will soon cascade into the coffers.

Cows moo of prosperity and tranquil times ahead. Enjoy them while they last – the herd may soon move on to pastures new.

Crowns say that honours are about to rain down on the questioner; not just honours, but maybe a legacy along with the chances of a dream coming true.

Daffodils are a welcome harbinger not just of spring, but of wealth waiting just around the corner.

Daggers warn of danger, especially if impetuous actions are taken. They can also suggest that a sudden shock could be in store, one brought about by the plotting of enemies.

Dice are a sign that now is the time to take a risk and wait for the good times to roll in.

Dogs, being famed for their qualities of friendship and loyalty, when seen in the teacup say that good friends are coming the querent's way, especially if they seem to be running towards the handle.

Donkeys are a sign that says, 'Be patient and things will work out.'

Doors offer a potentially exciting step into the unknown that can be taken with confidence if the door is open, but not if the door is closed as the passage floor on the other side of the door is not yet ready to be trodden upon.

Dots, as well as speaking of money-making opportunities, also underline the meaning of any nearby symbol.

Ducks brings with them the chance perhaps to travel by water and of opportunity swimming in from abroad. Ducks can also say that if the querent has been searching to find his natural role in life, the search may soon be over.

Drums have quarrels and disagreements, scandal and gossip in their beat, and to see them in the teacup is a call to action.

Ears are a sign that the questioner should be on the alert because malicious rumours are being spread about him: or if they are not already, they soon will be.

Eggs signify an increase of some kind, perhaps springing from a new project.

Egg-timers say that if the querent is faced with completing a task of some sort, time may be running out.

Elephants are a good thing to see, signifying wisdom and a success, maybe thanks to the efforts of a trustworthy friend.

Envelopes bring with them news of some kind in the cup just as the letters they contain do in life – the main difference being that in the cup, they always mean some kind of good news.

Eyes are a warning to act carefully over the coming weeks.

Faces, when they are smiling, are a sign of happiness: but when frowning they say that opposition will soon stand in the way of any progress in the querent's life.

Fans herald flirtation, maybe leading to some sort of indiscretion.

Feathers are a sign that indiscretion and instability will upset the questioner in some way – but not too seriously.

Feet suggest that an important decision will have to be made in the near future and that if it is to lead to success, then the querent will have to act quickly. Feet also say that if he is to find success, he may have to look way beyond his own backyard to find it.

Fences – a warning that limitations are about to be imposed that will restrict the querent's options, perhaps because someone is being overprotective.

Fingers – when pointing to another sign, this emphasizes the second sign's meaning.

Fingernails point towards unfair accusations being made.

Fish bring with them some sort of good fortune, often the result of lucky speculation. They can also indicate that foreign travel is on the horizon.

Flags bring with them a warning of danger in the air, and suggest that to overcome it the querent will need to rally resources and act courageously.

Flies bring little domestic irritations, nothing serious, just constantly irksome things that will annoy the querent for some time to come.

Flowers, either a single bloom or a lovely bunch, presage a celebration of some sort. Flowers also signify that the questioner will be showered with small kindnesses that
will make life worth living. One bloom can mean that love is about to appear, several that if the questioner is about to face an interview, there is nothing to worry about. If the flowers take the form of a garland, then recognition and promotion lie ahead.

Forks are a warning to beware flattery and false friends.

Fountains say that success lies in store for the querent. They also indicate that he or she is more interested in sexual passion than romantic love.

Foxes signify sagacity and foresight. They tell the querent that if she cannot achieve her aims by using persuasion, there is nothing wrong with subtlety or even stealth, but not at the expense of honesty.

Frogs are an indication that the questioner has the happy knack of fitting in no matter where he is. Frogs can also presage some sort of change, perhaps a change of address.

Fruit is a sign of prosperous times in store (see also Apples and Grapes).

Gallows warn that a loss is about to hit: it might be a financial one, or it could be that someone who was a good friend is about to be crossed off the querent's Christmas-card list. They can also suggest that the querent is feeling locked in a potentially dangerous situation from which they can see no means of escape – but desperately want to find one. Conversely, if the questioner is not in the best of health, gallows are a sign of an upturn.

Gates can be good or bad, depending on whether they are open or closed. When open, prosperity and happiness lie ahead. But when barring the way ahead then they should be taken as a warning to be on guard against a loss of some kind, financial maybe or perhaps a valued possession is about to take wing.

Geese are not the most common of birds seen in the teacup, but if one or more is recognized, take it as a signal to heed any warnings that are issued in the near future. Doing so will save a situation: ignore them at your peril.

Giants foretell that a person with a magnetic and dominant personality is about to loom into view. Giants also suggest that huge strides will be made on the career front.

Grapes presage prosperity, a sign to squeeze every ounce of opportunity from chances that are about to present themselves. They are a sign of good health and an augury that this is the time to indulge yourself and give yourself a chance to make your dreams come true.

Grass suggests that something, an inner restlessness perhaps, is about to cause discontent, often with something that has to do with a long-term, but still developing situation with which the querent is involved.

Guitars presage great harmonious riffs, perhaps leading to romance. But they can also indicate a vain nature and a tendency to being irritable with those whom the querent considers to be of inferior talent.

Guns say that if other people's inertia has been harnessing progress, then now is the time to cut the ties that bind. Guns are also a warning that unless properly channelled, an outburst of aggression may have unfortunate results.

Hammocks, with their associations with long summer days spent snoozing, suspended between two trees, suggest an unconventional nature and perhaps a desire to opt out of responsibilities and take things easy.

Hands that are open and outstretched say that a new friendship is about to be forged – and that it will be mutually beneficial. If they are closed, though, someone is about to act in a very mean way, which is quite out of character.

Hats are a signal that change is the air, perhaps in the shape of a new job. Headgear can also herald the arrival of an unexpected visitor (some believe that it will be an old rival making an unexpected reappearance) or that an invitation to a formal occasion may turn up in the post.

Heads offer a hint to be on the lookout for new opportunities that could result in a promotion to a new position of authority.

Hearts whisper that a new friendship is around the corner, indeed it could already have presented itself: and it could be one that might lead to romance and, who knows, marriage. Hearts also indicate that a family situation is developing that will need to be handled with tremendous tact and sensitivity if it is not to end in a rift.

Hens cluck that an older person, probably a motherly type, will come to have an increasing influence in the querent's life, but that her over-fussiness will become more and more irritating.

Hills should be taken as a warning that the path ahead may become blocked, but the problems will be little ones and easily overcome and when they are, long-term ambitions will be achieved. If they seem to be shrouded in mist, take this as an indication of uncertainty over which of the mutually exclusive options that present themselves should be taken.

Horns are a welcome sign, cornucopias that will bring with them an abundance of happiness and peace.

Horses bring news of a lover, especially if just the head is seen. They are also a sign of good news generally. If they are at full stretch, galloping across the cup, they indicate that it may be time to saddle up and get travelling. If they are seen harnessed to a cart then they signify that a change of job or address is beckoning – a very advantageous one if the cart is full.

Horseshoes herald the same good luck in the cup as they did in the days when one found in a lane or byway was hung up above the front door to encourage good fortune.

Houses can indicate that there is nothing to fear in the days immediately ahead, for they bring security with them. But they can also say that domestic matters are about to take up an increasing amount of time.

Icebergs are a sign that someone the querent knows has hidden depths and that if they are not recognized there could be trouble in store.

Igloos say that seeking some sort of refuge from an emotional situation might be OK as long as it is recognized that doing so is a temporary measure and must not become permanent.

Initials represent the people for whom they stand and say that the signs closest refer to them rather than the querent.

Ink spilt in the cup represent doubts that must be clarified before the querent signs an important document, probably a legal one.

Inkpots, like ink, can have a legal aspect, indicating as they do that there are important legal or official matters to be communicated in writing.

Insects suggest little problems will irritate the querent – nothing serious, though, just thoroughly annoying, like a buzzing bluebottle that you keep swatting but never manage to get.

Islands have a duality of meanings. On the one hand, they can suggest that a holiday, to an exotic location perhaps, is coming up. On the other hand they can say that the querent is feeling increasingly isolated, probably in some matter on the work front.

Jewels say that someone is about to bestow an unexpected gift of a very generous nature on the querent.

Jugs are a sign that life is about to be brimful with good health if it is not so already. That's if they are full. Empty ones are a warning that money is being frittered away on unnecessary little luxuries.

Kettles whistle of domestic happiness – as long as they are near the handle. But if they are near the bottom of the cup, then the opposite holds true.

Keys are a sign of enlightenment and of new opportunities unless (and there is so often an 'unless' in reading the leaves) there are two of them at the bottom of the cup. If so, lock the doors and fasten the windows, for they warn of a burglary. They also signify an increasingly independent nature, perhaps of a child about to flee the nest.

Kings can warn that an older person may act in a high-handed manner that could be very upsetting. But it could be that he (or she) is acting out of a genuine desire to help and should be regarded as an ally – a very powerful one.

Kites, soaring around the cup, speak of lofty aspirations being successfully achieved.

Knives warn that a relationship is about to come to an end – the closer they are to the top of the cup, the closer that relationship will be. At the very top, then divorce is in the air. At the bottom, then lawsuits beckon – the closer to the bottom, the more acrimony will they bring in their wake. Anywhere else, they say, 'Beware of false friends!'

Ladders suggest that an advancement of some sort will present itself to the querent. It could be promotion at work, or it could be something more spiritual. They are also a sign that this is the time to set sights high.

Leaves are a welcome sign that good fortune is about to smile, bringing prosperity in its wake. Falling leaves hint that, come the autumn, some sort of natural turning point will be reached that will bring a surge of happiness.

Letters, the sort contained in envelopes, bring with them news from afar.

Lines have different meanings, depending on whether they are straight, slanting or curvy. Straight ones suggest progress in life, perhaps through a journey. Slanting lines speak of failure in business. And curved, wavy ones herald disappointments and uncertainty lying in wait.

Lions – the kings of the jungle signify powerful friends.

Lizards were scurrying around long before our ancestors descended from the trees, and as such are a sign to get in touch with primitive instincts and to trust them. They are also a warning to check all facts extremely carefully as   the source may not be as reliable as it seems.

Looms see **Spinning wheels**.

Loops indicate that the path ahead is a crooked one; the end is in sight, but getting there is going to take forever as pointless disagreements and unwise decisions are going to make the journey seem interminable.

Magnets mean that a new interest will become increasingly important – and it could well be a romantic interest, meeting someone who is magnetically attractive and absolutely irresistible.

Maps can say that a desire to travel will soon be satisfied or that well-laid plans will give life a new destination. They can also signify that, after a long period of uncertainty, life gets back on an even keel.

Maypoles, once a common sight at spring fairs, indicate that new life is stirring after a period of dormancy. They also might herald news of a pregnancy or that a project started in the spring will come to a happy conclusion.

Men mean visitors, and if their arms are outstretched, then they are bearing gifts, so welcome them.

Mermaids sing that passion will lead to temptation and temptation to infidelity and infidelity to heartbreak.

Mice, peeking out from among the leaves, squeak of oncoming poverty, perhaps as the result of theft. They also say that this is not the time to be timid about anything and that if the initiative is taken, the benefits will be substantial.

Mirrors might indicate that the querent is of a vain nature or that they feel that life is passing them by.

Moles suggest that secrets are in the air and that when they are revealed they will have a significant effect on the questioner's life. These 'little gentlemen in velvet waistcoats' can also point to the fact that a false friend is doing something that will undermine the querent in some way.

The Moon is one of the most often-seen symbols in the cup. If it is a full one (moon that is, not cup) then a love affair is in the offing. If it is a waxing moon, then new projects will prosper, and if it is waning then a decline in fortune is indicated. If it is partially obscured, then, sadly, depression is about to cloud the querent's life. And if it is surrounded by what look like little dots, tiny fragments of tea leaves, then marriage is in the air – but for money, rather than love.

Monks see **Nuns**.

Mountains can be a sign that obstacles, more serious ones than those indicated by hills, will appear and block the querent's view of the future. But they also stand for high ambitions that may or may not be achieved, depending on what else is in the cup.

Nails suggest that the querent is about to be hammered by malice, pain and injustice. That said, to get what is due, the querent will have to fight hard.

Necklaces suggest a secret admirer who, when he presents himself, may turn out to be the 'one'. A broken necklace, though, warns of a friendship that may be about to cool unless care is taken.

Needles have a trilogy of meanings. They can say that a quarrel is about to be settled to everyone's satisfaction. They might suggest that the best way to deal with jealous criticism is to brush it to one side. And lastly, if there's a needle in the cup an unsatisfactory situation is being tolerated in the hope that something will turn up to make things better.

Nests say that domestic matters are about to come to the fore and that someone is about to ask for the key to the door and become a visitor rather than a resident.

Nets can be taken as a sign that the questioner is feeling trapped or maybe worried about a new venture. They can also be taken to mean that something that has long been looked for is about to present itself.

Numbers, close to a leaf or leaves that indicate an upcoming event in the querent's life, tell the number of days that will elapse before that event will occur. Some numbers, though, have their own meanings. One signposts creativity, energy and new beginnings. Two is a sign of duality and rivalry, while three sometimes promises a betrothal. Four says that now is the time to accept that resources are limited and to work within them. Five is a sign that clear communication is needed when dealing with others. Six heralds peaceful and harmonious times. Seven points towards the unconscious world and says that it is now the time to put things into long-term perspective. Eight cautions the querent to follow convention, while nine suggests self-interest, as well as being a sign of a project being completed satisfactorily.

Nuns are indicative of a desire to go into retreat and withdraw from life for a while to ponder upon the best way to achieve a path that satisfies the material and the spiritual. The holy sisters can also represent wise friends who are always in the wings, waiting to help whenever called upon.

Oars say that the time has come to stop waiting for others to help and find a solution to whatever ails, perhaps by moving to a new house or new job.

Octopuses suggest that danger is about to entwine the querent in its tentacles, probably because he or she has overstretched available resources and taken on too much either in business or in personal life. On a happier note, they can also represent a multi-talented person who will be only too happy to oblige.

Ostriches, well known for burying their heads in the sand when danger threatens, say that the questioner shares that particular trait.

Owls warn that there's trouble perched on a nearby branch, ready to swoop down at any moment. The trouble in question could be brought about by gossip and scandal, or perhaps a failure of some sort. They also warn of neglected tasks. But they have a good meaning, too, signifying that a very wise person is standing by to help.

Oysters promise that the querent has hidden depths and talents that, if plumbed and used at the right time, will be of tremendous benefit to all.

Padlocks, when they are open offer the promise of the chance to get out of a difficult situation or to get out of an unwanted arrangement. When they are closed, then unspoken concerns about a job or a domestic matter are starting to bring their weight to bear.

Palaces see **Castles**.

Palm trees say that success will bring honour to the questioner, who may well be feeling a need to be cherished by family and friends. And being trees with exotic associations, they may be a sign that travel to an exotic place is on the horizon.

Parachutes announce that help is at hand if the querent is feeling vulnerable in any way. They can also mean that fear of failure or impending disaster can be dismissed for this is completely unfounded.

Parrots say that needless chatter and trivialities are clouding real issues. These talkative birds also warn that passing on gossip could have far-reaching and unfortunate results.

Peacocks promise that the querent's desire for a more luxurious lifestyle may be about to be fulfilled and if they are feeling proud at some recent achievement then quite right too. But they can also say that the vanity of friends poses a threat in some way.

Pendulums signify that the questioner needs to put some effort into restoring harmony with family, friends and colleagues. Another meaning is that there is a change of course on the cards, and a third is a warning not to take things at face value, to look below the surface to establish the reality of a situation.

Pigs might represent a generous, extremely hospitable friend, or they can warn that overindulgence could lead to ill health.

Pigeons may be an annoying fact of urban living but in tasseography they suggest that an unexpected communication will be received from far-off places, and that the bearer of the news is someone in whom the querent can have absolute confidence.

Pipes suggest that if careful thought is given to a problem, the solution will waft its way into the querent's mind.

Pistols warn of danger and that someone will use unpleasant methods to get their own way at the expense of the questioner.

Precipices see **Cliffs**.

Purses presage luck or gain, depending on whether they are open or shut. They tend to turn up frequently in the cups of people who have deep pockets and short arms.

Pyramids indicate a concern with healing and psychic powers. If they appear in the leaves of someone who the reader knows has a pressing problem, then the answer to it lies in the past not in the present.

Question marks suggest that hesitancy and caution should be the watchwords for the coming days.

Rabbits say that speed is of the essence, especially if there are enemies to confront. And with their association with being prolific breeders, they can also indicate that the querent is concerned with fertility in some way.

Rainbows signify that while some wishes may be about to be fulfilled, other, more unrealistic ones, may have to be put on hold.

Rats warn the querent to be on the lookout for a vindictive, deceitful person who has revenge in mind. On a brighter note, they might be saying that if open-handed methods have failed the querent, then now might be the time to try underhand ones!

Ravens suggest that a warning of some sort may be about to be issued, and that while it may be unwelcome, it would be extremely foolhardy to ignore it. And if the querent has been told something in confidence, it would also be unwise to break it.

Rings, if they are close to the top, mean that marriage is immediately around the corner. In the middle, then a proposal can be expected in the near, but not immediate future. If it is at the bottom then the engagement will be a long one, a very long one. The marriage that takes place, be it tomorrow, next year or several years down the line, will be a happy one if the ring is complete. If it is broken, then the marriage won't be happy or unhappy: the engagement will be broken off before the bride walks down the aisle.

Roads suggest that a new path is about to appear in the questioner's life. If they are straight, fine. But a fork suggests that a choice will have to be made – the wider the fork, the more important the choice.

Rocks strew the path ahead with obstacles and hazards. But all is not bad news, for they can be overcome without too much difficulty, and more positively, it may be that they can be used as building bricks or stepping stones to a better future with a little careful thought.

Scales, of the weighing rather than the fishy kind, are a sign of justice and judgement. In Ancient Egypt, after a death, the heart of the deceased was weighed against a feather to find out if they qualified for the afterlife.

The oncoming judgement foretold by scales in the cup will not have such an eternal result – but it could be significant just the same. Balanced ones suggest a just, fair decision will bring benefits, unbalanced ones that the questioner will suffer through injustice.

Scissors presage domestic arguments and worse that they will become so bitter that separation is on the cards.

Seesaws can mean that mood swings will see the querent lightheaded with happiness one minute, down in the dumps the next. They can also indicate that the swings and roundabouts of life will make it hard to achieve a proper sense of balance.

Sharks say that some force may be required if attacks from an unexpected source are to be repelled with any chance of success.

Shells mean that good news is coming in with the tide. They also indicate intuitive wisdom and tell the questioner not only to listen to the inner voice that is called instinct, but to act on it.

Ships can say that an increase is on the horizon. They can also suggest that if the querent is worried about something they can cast any doubts overboard, because it will come to a successful conclusion.

Snakes have the well-known ability to shed their skins. Their appearance in the teacup suggests that it is time for the querent to, metaphorically speaking, get rid of current burdens and responsibilities and slide, regenerated, towards the future.

Spiders suggest to some readers that someone is spinning a web of subterfuge that will soon enmesh the questioner. To others it says that persistence will pay off financially.

Spinning wheels say two things. The good news is that they say that careful planning and consistent industry will bring good results. The bad news is that they can point to the fact that someone is plotting behind the scenes to the querent's detriment.

Squares were once seen as signs of some sort of restriction, but are now generally taken to mean that protection is there for the asking, if need be. They also say that if the querent uses the near future to lay down some careful long-term plans, it will lead to a boost of financial and material prospects.

Squirrels, as one might expect, carry the message that people who save for the future have less to worry about than spendthrifts who live for today and to hell with tomorrow.

Stars can shine with messages of hope, particularly where health matters are concerned. If they have five points, good fortune in general is there for the asking. But if the star is an eight-pointed one, accidents will cause reversals. If there are five stars a-twinkling in the cup, then success will come, but it will not bring any happiness. And seven stars say that grief may be about to strike.

The Sun says that the grey skies of disappointment will soon clear and happiness will beam down on the querent, bringing with it success and perhaps power. The Sun can mean, too, that the next summer will be an especially happy one, perhaps involving travel to a sunny destination.

Swords suggest that the querent should prepare himself for quarrels and disputes.

Tables indicate that social life is about to take a lively and positive upturn.

Teapots presage meetings – long, boring ones which will make the querent come to the widely held belief that any meeting of more than two people is a complete waste of time.

Telescopes say that the answers to present mysteries will soon be revealed, but that the answers lie outside the immediate environment.

Tents indicate a love of adventure, but one that could lead to an unsettled life.

Tortoises with their associations with longevity say that while success can be achieved, it will be a long time a-coming. They also indicate a love of tradition.

Towers can imply that the querent is feeling restricted in some way, unless they have steps, in which case they lead to a rise in status and a boost to the finances. A tower that is incomplete suggests that plans are not yet finished – and never will be.

Trees augur a growth in prosperity, brought about by long-held ambitions coming to happy fruition. Romany folk believe that if the tree is surrounded by smaller leaves, then these ambitions will be realized in the country, or at least they will be associated with it in some way.

Triangles can mean unexpected success or unexpected failure, depending on the way the triangle is pointing. Upwards is good; downwards bad, unless the querent realizes that there is still time to grab an opportunity that is just about to slip from his grasp.

Tunnels promise that present confusion and setbacks will soon be swept away, but only if the querent probes in the right places.

Turtles see **Tortoises**.

Umbrellas suggest that little annoyances are about to shower on the questioner. They also signify a need for shelter. If they are open, then that shelter will be found; if the umbrella is rolled up, then it will not be.

Unicorns offer the promise of magical insights that illumine the querent's life in some way. They also promise that unusual and unexpected opportunity is on the horizon.

Vans bring movement in their wake.

Violins see **Guitars**.

Volcanoes presage that an eruption of passion will soon sweep the querent off her feet. They often appear when the person whose leaves are being read is one who is seething with anger, but is determined not to let it show.

Walking sticks herald the arrival of a visitor.

Waterfalls bring prosperity with them.

Weathervanes point to inconsistent and indecisive friends. They warn the querent to be on the lookout for signs of change that, if recognized and acted on when the time is right, will lead to some benefit.

Webs, like their weaver, the spider, are a sign that deceit and subterfuge will have a significant bearing on the querent's life.

Whales promise the successful fulfilment of a big undertaking. They offer commercial and professional success, the latter especially if the querent is involved in one of the caring professions.

Wheels, if they are complete, say that good fortune is about to roll in. If they are near the rim of the cup, then the good fortune will come in the form of an unexpected legacy or win of some sort. But if the wheel is broken then disappointments loom.

Windows can mean good luck or bad luck depending on whether they are open or shut. They may offer new insights or a chance to explore new horizons, unless they are curtained, in which case they point to the fact that other people's narrow horizons are holding the querent back in some way.

3

CRYSTAL DIVINATION

Think of divination and one of the stereotypical images that probably comes to mind is that of an old crone peering into a crystal ball and making relevant what she sees in it to whichever question has been put to her. Not something to be taken seriously. Something that whiled away half an hour on a rainy afternoon during a traditional British seaside holiday in the days before cheap foreign travel whisked us off to sunnier destinations.

This image of the crystal gazer has probably done more to harm divination's reputation than any other, which is sad because crystal gazing has a long and honourable tradition as part of scrying – using crystals, mirrors, flames and water as a means to peer into the future.

Crystal gazing has its roots in prehistory, when the tribe member who was credited with the gift of seeing peered into a reflective surface to discern what lay around the corner. It was not necessarily a crystal: a stretch of calm, still water served the purpose just as well.

In slightly more modern times, Nostradamus, the famous seer whose prophesies continue to unfold many centuries after his death, would sit alone at night, gazing into a bowl of water held in a brass tripod and lit by a candle. In the mirror-like surface he saw his visions, that are still relevant in our lifetime. His English contemporary, Dr John Dee, whose divinatory talents were recognized by Queen Elizabeth I, used a shiny black obsidian mirror to help in his prophesying.

Traditionally, the ball used for crystal gazing should be a gift from someone with the talent, but nowadays they are easily available in a variety of crystals – clear or smoky quartz, beryl and obsidian are the most popular – and glass from specialist shops. Glass ones should be examined particularly closely for any blemishes or bubbles that could be distracting.

When buying one, the mood should be relaxed and receptive, an atmosphere encouraged in spiritual shops not just by the incense that is often burned there, but by the positive vibrations given off by staff and fellow customers. Handle several crystal balls, which are usually about four inches (ten centimetres) in diameter. How do they fit in the hand? Are they perfectly plain spheres or do they have angles and planes within them? Most people find that when they go to buy their crystal ball, they keep returning to one, no matter how many they look at and handle. If this happens, that is the ball to buy.

To prepare the ball, wash it in a mild solution of vinegar and water, then polish it with a soft cloth. When it is not being used, the ball should be wrapped in a cloth to keep it out of direct sunlight, which affects sensitivity: and it should not be handled by anyone other than the user. Some gazers unwrap their crystal ball and put it in a moonlit place during a full Moon, which they believe enhances the crystal's power.

Crystals pick up vibrations when handled by other people. If someone else is to handle another's crystal ball, the hands must be cupped around it, and after use, the ball should either be washed in vinegar or water, or held under running water while visualizing it surrounded with bright, shining light. That done, it should be wrapped in silk or velvet until it is to be used again.

How they work

When gazing into a crystal ball, intuition should be focused, the rational mind suspended. Soft, gentle light reflects off the crystal, catching the eye and holding it firm.

It's not long before the eyes go slightly out of focus, the ball mists over and within the mist images start to form. These images are projections from the gazer's mind or inner crystal.

The room should be quiet, a place where the gazer will not be disturbed, and gently lit, in the words of one gazer, 'like daylight on a wet, cloudy day'. Some people use candlelight to achieve this, others swathe the lamps with a suitable (flame-retardant) cloth.

It is essential that the gazer is in a relaxed state of mind before beginning: some people can achieve this by deep breathing, others use visualizing techniques. As this is being achieved, the crystal should be held in the hands for a few moments to attune the ball to the gazer's vibrations. At the same time, questions can be framed, and safe solutions considered but not pondered on too deeply.

The ball is now placed on a black silk or velvet cloth, and perhaps partially surrounded with a black velvet or silk curtain or screen. Now stare at the crystal, until the eyes go out of focus, the mist forms and images appear within it. These images must not be forced: they should arise naturally. The images may appear in the ball or in the mind's eye. Even meaningless ones might have significance, so write everything down as it arises.

It takes time and concentration to gaze successfully into the crystal. But not too much time, and learning to concentrate properly is a talent that has many other applications, so it is well worth the effort. The first occasion should last no longer than ten minutes, gradually increasing the time of each session, at first to fifteen minutes, then twenty and so on, but no session should ever last longer than one hour. Time each session with a watch or clock positioned so that you can see its face, but will not be distracted by its ticking.

The presence of another person distracts concentration, at least at first. With experience comes the ability to answer the questions of others, as long as they are asked in a low, hushed voice.

Gazers often find that small glittering points of light appear in the mist, before the mist clears, and what has been described as an ocean of blue space appears, within which visions appear. These visions are sometimes symbolic, the meaning of the symbols being similar to those seen in a tea leaf reading (see pages xx-xx), or they may be scenic. Visions that appear in the background lie further ahead than those that are to the front, which denote the present or the immediate future.

When images come, no effort should be made to keep them there: they should be allowed to come and go, ebbing and flowing like the tide, with no attempt being made to control them.

Crystal clear

Crystal-ball reading is not the only use to which crystals can be put for divination. An assortment of small crystals kept in a special bag can also be used. The simplest way is to shake the bag, and while focusing on the question to be asked, take out the first two or three that the fingers touch. As they are drawn, take a moment or two to see if the answer comes spontaneously to mind, before looking up the meaning of the crystals.

More complex questions can be answered and guidance for the future gained by using crystals in any suitable Tarot spread. And boards on to which crystals are thrown are available from specialist shops: the combination of the answers on the board and the sagacity of the crystals have satisfied countless users.

Generally, red, yellow, orange and sparkling-white (hot-coloured) stones contain a great deal of creative energy and indicate that some action is indicated with regard to the area with which the particular stone is associated. Green, blue, purple, pink and pearly white stones reflect spiritual desires, thoughts and emotions.

The associations of some of the more common crystals used for this purpose are as follows:

Agate: Success in worldly matters
Amethyst: Shifts in consciousness and life changes
Black agate: Prosperity and courage
Blue lace agate: A need for healing
Red agate: Longevity and good health
Aventurine: Growth and expansion
Citrine: Wisdom in celestial matters
Diamond: Permanence
Emerald: Fertility
Jade: Immortality and perfection
Red jasper: Worldly affairs
Lapis lazuli: Favoured by the divine
Clear quartz: Self-healing and love
Sapphire: Chastity and truth
Snowflake obsidian: Closure of a challenging time
Tiger's eye: The need to look beneath the surface
White quartz: Change of a profound nature
Unakite: Integration and composure

NUMEROLOGY

Pythagoras, the founder of geometry, asserted that numbers were the essence of all things. Each one, he taught his students at his school at Crotone in Italy, had its own, unique vibration and specific personality. And it was he who divided the human soul into nine different types, the numbers of which are still used today.

There is also a symbiotic connection between numbers and astrology, which has been with us for centuries. Each astrological sign is assigned a planet and a corresponding number, which, it can be assumed, have similar attributes.

For historical reasons, the Sun and the Moon are allocated two numbers because, when the system was devised, there were only seven known planets and nine numbers to be allocated.

Numerology is concerned only with the numbers one to nine, to which all other numbers are reduced. Zero is not a number in numerology terms. It adds nothing at the beginning of a sequence and adds nothing to any other digit to which it is attached. The number ten exists as a composite of the number one (1 + 0 = 1). All subsequent numbers are treated in the same way.

Sun sign	Ruling planet	Number
Aries	Mars	9
Taurus	Venus	6
Gemini	Mercury	5
Cancer	Moon	2/7
Leo	Sun	1/4
Virgo	Mercury	5
Libra	Venus	6
Scorpio	Mars	9
Sagittarius	Jupiter	8
Aquarius	Saturn	8
Pisces	Jupiter	3

The Birth Number

This is the number that reveals natural powers and abilities. It is often used as an indication of likely career choices. To calculate this number the individual components of the subject's date of birth are written down and then reduced to a single number. Thus, a person born on 16 November 1945 would have a birth number of 1, calculated as follows:

1 + 6 + 1 + 1 (November is the eleventh month) + 1 + 9 + 4 + 5 = 28.
Being a composite number, 28 is broken down to 2 + 8 = 10
And 10 being a composite number is broken down to 1 + 0 = 1.

1. The associations of this number with the Sun and the fire signs Leo, Sagittarius and Aries spell leadership. In many religions it is the number of resurrection and being the first number, rising from the chaos of nothing, it is linked with new beginnings, breaks with the past and with limitless energy. It is often linked with assertiveness and masculinity.

   People whose birth number is one are often striking to look at, with a mane of fair hair, a lean, athletic body and with beautiful skin that tans glowingly and quickly. They reflect an aura of good health and wellbeing and are usually perceived to be physically attractive with aesthetically pleasing features. The overall impression created by those with this number is one of action, fitness and general good health.

   But, being a young number, one can bring with it immaturity and a tendency to sulkiness, especially towards those who spurn attempts to be led. One people need loyalty and when they don't get it, they feel slighted.

2. Linked to the Moon, now a symbol of femininity, two brings with strong intuition, the power of deep thought and attractive sensitivity. Men with two as their birth number are often closely in touch with their feminine side, and twos of both sexes are often fair skinned with pale, lustreless blonde hair and a dislike of bright sunshine. They may have a slight physique and show a tendency to underestimate themselves, something that leads to them having difficulties in standing their ground.

   They are often so quietly spoken that one has to strain to hear what they say. But they have a tendency to say one thing and do another, something that often causes difficulties in maintaining relationships.

3. A mystical number in many cultures, as witnessed by the Holy Trinity of the Christian faith. Chinese philosophers believed that three was the number from which creatures that embraced the Yin and the Yang were created. People whose birth number is

three are usually uncommonly intelligent and wise: they love life and have a strong sense of the sensual. The solid physique of youth can easily give over to fat in middle age, if care is not taken.

Threes have outgoing personalities and share a dislike of their own company. They often have psychic abilities and love acquiring knowledge.

4. Another Sun number, which in many cultures is symbolized by the serpent. Four people often have a tough, aggressive nature but keep it hidden under the well-balanced façade they present to the world. They enjoy hard work and the rewards it brings. They have tough bodies and quick, alert minds, but are often diffident when it comes to starting relationships because of a curious lack of confidence. But make friends with a four and you have a friend for life. That said, remember the dragon that lurks beneath the surface and be careful not to stir it.

5. The number of the planet Mercury, messenger to the gods and child of Maia after whom the fifth month, May, is named. Fives are mentally and physically always on the move. They are often slender of build and find it hard to put on weight, thanks to the effect their constant hurrying and scurrying has on their fast metabolism.

They have persuasive tongues, especially when it comes to sex for they can charm the birds off the trees and whoever they set their sights at into bed. And cheerful extroverts they may be, but they can be anxious and impatient. Also, their incessant movement often disguises prevarication: actually getting things done is quite a different thing from looking busy.

Their agile minds make fives good inventors. Their fertile imaginations make them good authors. Their behaviour may suggest genius: but it might just as easily say deluded. That's the trouble with fives. As Bernard Shaw wrote, 'You never can tell, sir, you never can tell.'

6. Venus's number, six is the symbol of partnership, love and marriage. Those whose birth number it is can be fairly certain that they will enjoy loving and fruitful relationships. Blessed with good figures, their love of the good things in life might lead to a tendency to the sort of plumpness that was once fashionable, but which is now frowned upon in the lean times in which we live.

   With their attractive bright eyes, six people have pleasing manners, are outgoing and friendly. But they can also be curiously introverted and enjoy the company of quiet, artistic people. They are home-loving people who enjoy looking good, something that can make them appear overdressed.

7. There are seven days in the week, seven colours in the rainbow, seven pillars of wisdom, seven branches on the Jewish menorah: seven is perhaps the most magical of the nine single-digit numbers with which numerology is concerned.

   Seven people, though, are not so magical by nature (and are often not very tall in stature either). They are realists who are not preoccupied with appearance and superficiality, but instead prefer to cultivate a warm and cheerful disposition.

   Sevens are often very friendly and make great company. They enjoy nothing more than seeing others enjoy themselves as much as they do.

8. With Saturn its associated planet, eight is the number of secret, dark places.

   It is symbolic of the good aspects of old age – wisdom and patience – and the unfortunate ones – regret, disillusionment and failing health.

   People whose birth number is eight are often tall and slender of build. Not that you will notice, for smiling is not something that Saturnine eights are prone to do often.

   They mature earlier than their peers, something that makes them liable to express their opinions in an overly forthright way. But the strong ideals that they have and their strong principles often encourage others to seek their advice, something that will be given in the cold, dispassionate way that is typical of the eight person.

9. Mars, god of war, rules nine, the number of wisdom and virtue – and their opposites – ignorance and profligacy.

Nine people often have powerful physiques, ruddy complexions and dark hair. They share a tendency to have facial hair and to have been born with unfortunate birthmarks.

Coming before ten, which reduces to one, nine rekindles the lifespark. This makes nines confident, often overconfident, which is something that can lead to their being impetuous and accident-prone. And while they can be full of vitality and enthusiasm, ambitious and energetic, they can also be insecure and quarrelsome, slapdash and autocratic.

The Destiny Number

This number shows life's purpose, the opportunities that will present themselves and how they should be used to achieve optimum potential. In calculating the Destiny Number, each letter of the full birth name is ascribed a number. These are then added together and treated as above until a single number is reached.

Thus someone named at birth Michael Mitchell Johnstone would calculate his Destiny Number as follows:

$$4 + 9 + 3 + 8 + 1 + 5 + 3 + 4 + 9 + 2 + 3 + 8 + 5 + 3 + 3 + 1 +$$
$$6 + 8 + 5 + 1 + 2 + 6 + 5 + 5 = 109 = 1 + 0 + 9 = 10 = 1 + 0$$
$$= 1$$

The name can also be used for more refined readings. By reducing the numerical values of just the vowels of any name to a single numeral we get a number (the Name Vowel Number) that gives an indication that some say represents the Freudian ego – the exposed, conscious outer self. Correspondingly, the Name Consonant Number, calculated using only the numerical values of the consonants, represents the Freudian id – the hidden, unconscious self.

Name Vowel Numbers

1   Suggests an open, confident personality, but perhaps someone who genuinely believes themselves to be better than their fellows. If this goes unchecked it might lead to selfishness and a tendency to offer the hand of friendship only to fawning acolytes. But ones are a gregarious group, who make friends easily and who enjoy money.

2   Often indicates a lack of self-confidence and a tendency to being perhaps just a little too laid back, but it also hints at great creative talents. If twos can get their act together, they often make excellent counsellors and caring members of the medical profession.

3   Points to a confident, extrovert nature, to people who enjoy the good things in life so much that they overindulge in them. Those with three as their Name Vowel Number are frank and honest to the point of bluntness. They are natural teachers with a thirst for learning, especially about the arts.

4   Says 'responsibility', 'dependability' and 'stability' but also 'self-doubt'. Four people claim to like freedom in their friendships and their jobs, but deep down they harbour a desire for a more structured existence. Emotionally, they tend to keep themselves to themselves. Professionally, they tend towards careers in the arts, architecture and design.

5   Is often the Name Vowel Number of clever, quick-minded people who enjoy learning languages and acquiring new skills. They may have quick tempers and be obsessive about cleanliness and punctuality. They keep emotional commitments at bay, but love a good gossip.

6   Is a number that suggests a well-balanced nature, perhaps a little reserved and maybe a little over-polite. Those with this number are upset by anything that is controversial, untidy or unjust. They may sit on the fence, seeing both sides of any argument, secretly longing to come down heavily in favour of one side, but holding back from doing so.

7   Encourages a bright, creative nature enjoyed by the sort of person who is always on the go, bouncing here, there and everywhere, and with a deep desire to please everyone at the same time. They can be intellectual but erratic, often starting ambitious schemes only to drop them when the first hurdle looms.

8   Indicates a conventional nature, someone who is stable and cautious, but with a lively imagination that occasionally shows itself in behaviour that surprises. People with this number don't like sudden change. They are often regarded as plodders, but they usually succeed in getting what they want, and then move on to something else.

9   Is a pugnacious Name Vowel Number, often that of the sort of person who sees things in black and white, with no shades of grey. They act first and think later, but their enthusiasm and generosity often makes those affected by their rash decisions forgive them quickly.

Name Consonant Numbers

1   Suggests a strong sense of one's own worth and the belief that one's own ideas are always the best on offer.
2   Indicates a prolific imagination and the tendency to live in a fantasy world.
3   Points to a sensual nature and a feeling that one's deeply held religious or psychic beliefs set one apart from one's fellows.

4 Says that a creative nature is married to common-sense but warns that persistence might be mistaken for donkey-like stubbornness.
5 May make those with this number restless and eccentric, which some may find appealing and others unbelievably annoying.
6 is a contemplative number, suggesting a liking for the meditative and the mystical and a dislike of change.
7 Is associated with an instinctive knowledge of how things are and how they should be, and a liking for one's own company.
8 Speaks of caution, an unwillingness to take risks and a dislike of waste. But it also has hints of sexual passion.
9 Is a number of deep desires often unfortunately coupled with an inability to express them, which often leads to dashed ambitions and unrealized dreams.

5

PALMISTRY

Palmistry is the marriage of two ancient disciplines – chirognomy, which studies what the shape and markings of the human hand, its texture and colour, tell us about the person's character; and chiromancy, which aims to use the information the hand holds to divine future events in life. (Hands can also indicate some diseases: red palms can be a sign of serious liver disease, for instance.)

Like so much of divination, palmistry was first practised in China more than 3,000 years ago (where it was, and remains, part of a larger attempt to see the identity of the 'correct path' by scrutinizing not just the hand but the face and forehead) and in India where it is closely linked to astrology.

Aristotle taught the ancient art of chirosophy (xier = the hand and sophia = wisdom) to Alexander the Great, who at one point had a great part of the civilized world in the palm of his hand.

In 315CE, six hundred years after Alexander died, a papal decree threatened excommunication or in extreme cases death, to anyone 'outside the Church', who practised palmistry. It was officially frowned upon during the reign of Henry VIII (r. 1509-47). As late as during the reign of George IV (r. 1820-30) it was decreed by the British parliament that 'Any person found practising palmistry is hereby deemed a rogue and a vagabond, to be sentenced to one year's imprisonment and to stand in the pillory.'

In Victorian times it came almost to be regarded as a science and was popular in upper-class salons, middle-class parlours and working-class kitchens. Oscar Wilde used palmistry as the theme of one of his stories, Lord Arthur Saville's Crime, in which during a party a palm reader tells the young Lord Arthur that it is his destiny that he (Lord Arthur) will commit murder. He does. At the end, driven to distraction by his fate, he kills the man who determined it.

Carl Jung, the famous psychologist, who studied introversion and extroversion, was fascinated by palmistry and his followers came to believe that the outward personality (the extrovert) is in the dominant hand and the inner one (the introvert) in the minor hand. The dominant hand reflects events that have happened and as they are unfolding now – achievements and disappointments, changes of opinion – with the three main lines (heart, head and life) representing the physical organs of the body. The minor hand can give an excellent insight into the subject's potential and what, deep down, they really want in life.

In this hand, the heart, head and life lines signify the energies, nervous and sexual, that drive the subject.

Palmistry, like so much of divination, depends on two things – trust between the palmist and the subject, and instinct. The reading should take place in a relaxed atmosphere rather than in a tent at the village fête! A shaded, room fragranced with suitable essential oils is ideal.

An introductory chat can tell the palmist a great deal about the subject: which is the dominant hand; does the subject gesticulate as she talks; are the hands open and relaxed, or are the fingers clenched into a fist; are the fingers adorned with rings. During this time, the reader might take the opportunity of taking the subject's hand in hers, looking at the texture, the colour, the condition of the fingernails and blemishes. And, one of the most important aspects of palmistry – the shape of the hand.

The actual reading can be done by examining the hand physically or by taking a palmprint. Either way, the hands being studied must be washed and thoroughly dried and free of rings.

To make a palmprint (one for each hand) you will need:

1. Acrylic Print-making ink (available from specialist shops).
2. A smooth metal or glass surface on which to roll out the ink.
3. A hard rubber roller (available from specialist shops or photographic supply shops).
4. Glossy paper.

Squeeze some ink onto the smooth surface and push the roller back and forth until it is evenly coated. Roll the roller over the hand to be printed, then position a piece of glossy paper on a soft or rubbery surface and carefully press the hand on to it gently. Now roll the hand off the paper towards the edge, so that the edge of the hand as well as the palm is printed. The subject may need reassuring that the ink comes off easily with soap.

Types of hands

Just as no two people, not even identical twins, have identical fingerprints, so no two people have exactly the same hands. That said, though, it is possible to identify six basic types of hand that can, in themselves, tell a great deal about the subject of the reading.

1. The normal or practical hand
This tends to be on the clumsy side with fingers that are short in comparison with the palm. People with this type of hand often lack patience and are quick to lose their temper. They also tend to be among the most passionate.

2. The square or elemental hand

People who have a tendency to being logical and, perhaps, creatures of habit often have square hands. They are also usually very helpful individuals who can be relied on in times of crisis. They are persistent to the point of doggedness, conventional, always above suspicion – and very often boring!

3. The spatulate hand

The hand and fingers of this type represent a fan, which indicates restlessness and excitability – the sort of person who can go from one extreme to another in the blink of an eye. Such people are often inventive with an original view of the world that enables them to make discoveries. They are risk-takers and good company, but can be slapdash and have a tendency to bend the rules more than it is wise to do.

4. The philosophical hand

These long, bony hands often belong to teachers, philosophers and intellectuals, who are always seeking the truth. The minutiae of life is of little concern to people with Philosophical Hands – they are far too easily distracted.

These are people who see the wider picture, often ignoring their immediate surroundings to the point that their untidiness borders on the eccentric.

5. The mixed hand

Neither one thing nor the other, this is probably the most difficult to interpret. Sometimes such a hand is clawed, something that indicates long-term anxiety over financial matters, or that the person is over-timid and cautious in everything he or she does.

6. The physic or pointed hand

Graceful and conic in shape with pointed, tapering fingers and a long palm, the Physic Hand suggests an intuitive person who is happy to follow his own instincts and is usually quite right to do so.

All fingers and thumbs

The first thing to look at is the thumb, which represents willpower, and see how it is held naturally. Insecure people tend to curl it up, defensively, within the palm. Then determine its size in proportion to the rest of the hand. When the lower knuckle of the dominant hand's thumb is placed at the bottom of the little finger, it should be about the same length as that finger.

Strong, thick, thumbs say that the sitter has the capacity to deal with whatever life throws in her direction. Long ones indicate rational, clear thinking and leadership qualities. People with short thumbs tend to be subordinate to stronger characters, lacking the will to resist them, which often makes them unhappy. Aggressive tendencies are shown by short stubby thumbs.

More information can be gleaned from the thumb's phalanges (the sections between the joints), which are read from the top down, the first one representing will and the lower one logic. They should be about the same length. If the lower one is longer, then its owner is probably someone who thinks and talks a lot – too much to get down to actually doing anything! If the upper phalange is longer, beware of a person who rushes head first into things and then cries for help as soon as any trouble threatens.

Low self-esteem is indicated by a flattened thumb pad and is something that often manifests itself in sexual promiscuity. A square tip indicates a practical nature, while a spatulate one shows that the owner is especially good with his hands.

The angle of the thumb to the index finger also yields significant information. If it is less than 45° the owner has a tendency to be something of a control freak. An angle of 90° between the two says that the person is a charming extrovert, outgoing and great company. Beware a thumb that curves significantly backwards: it sits in the hand of a killer in every sense of the word.

Each of the fingers is named, as follows. The first (index) finger, Jupiter, indicates ambition and expansion. The second finger, Saturn, is connected with judgement and knowledge. The third (ring) talks of exploits and achievements: it is the finger of Apollo. And the little finger, Mercury, is to do with observation and perception.

Generally, long fingers indicate that the person is something of a perfectionist, and extra-long ones say that he or she is prone to exaggeration. Short fingers indicate an impatient nature.

The Jupiter finger

A long index finger points to self-confidence and awareness. Its owner is ambitious and more than able enough to achieve these ambitions. A leader, this is a person to whom one can turn during any type of crisis. A medium-length one shows that its owner is confident when confidence is called for, and modest when being such is the order of the day. And whoever has a short index finger is shy, scared of failure, insecure and full of self-doubt.

The middle finger

A long middle finger talks of ambition without humour. Those with long middle fingers work hard to get ahead, and will surely do so. A medium-length one indicates that the owner has the maturity to know when it is time to work and when it is time to play. A short middle finger is a sign of a careless person who hates routine so much that disorganization is a word often used in his or her connection.

The ring finger

The finger often associated with creativity, a long one points to an artistic nature that often leads its owner into considering design, especially fashion design, as a career. It can also warn of a gambling streak. One of medium length still points to having a creative nature, but a more traditional, conservative one. A short ring finger means that there is little creativity in its owner's nature.

The little finger

Length here indicates intelligence and excellent communication skills that make their owners excellent writers and speakers. They might also have a stronger than average sex drive. A little finger that is medium in length says that the owner is of average intelligence – not too bright, but not particularly dim either. And a short one means emotional immaturity and a tendency towards gullibility and naïvety.

Length

The comparative length of the fingers are also indicative of a person's nature. When the first finger is longer than the ring one, this is indicative of someone who is driven by their ego. Religious leaders and senior officers in the services often have such fingers.

Where the second finger is flanked by index and ring fingers of equal length, the owner has a serious, controlled nature with a well-developed sense of curiosity.

If the third finger is longer than the index finger, then an emotional, intuitive nature is indicated, someone who makes a good doctor or nurse, and whose advice is always well worth listening to.

And if the little finger rises above the top joint of the ring finger, then this is a charismatic person with a quick wit and shrewd business abilities.

Shape

The shapes of the fingers are also significant. Square ones show a rational, methodical nature, someone who thinks a lot at the expense of creativity. Fingers that are pointed indicate a sensitive nature, fragile daydreamers who are often artists or writers. Someone with conical fingers is usually a person with a flexible nature who often has excellent negotiating skills and to whom emotional security is important, often over-important, to their well-being.

People with spatulate fingers can be exhaustingly active not just physically but intellectually: they are innovators and inventors, explorers and extroverts.

Fingernails

Fingernails, too, play their part in hand-reading. Square ones indicate an easy-going temperament, while broad ones say, 'Beware! I'm a strong character with an explosive temper!' Fan-shaped fingernails are a sign that the owner has been under some sort of stress for quite a long time. A gentle, kind nature is indicated by almond- shaped fingernails, but can say that the person is prone to daydreaming. A selfish, cold personality is shown by narrow nails. Wedge-shaped nails say that the person is oversensitive and as touchy as a nervous cat.

The nails can also indicate health problems. If they are dished, then the person's chemical balance is out of kilter. Dietary deficiencies may result in horizontal ridges forming in the nails: whereas rheumatism may cause vertical ones running down the nails.

The phalanges

These, the sections between the finger joints are read from the top down. The top one is concerned with introspection, the second corresponds to the subject's attitude to material concerns, and the third with physical desires.

The major lines of the palm

The lines that criss-cross the palms of the hand are just one of the things that professional palm-readers look at, whereas to the amateurs (and no disrespect to them) who do readings at village fêtes they are very often the only things that are considered. The professional interprets their meaning in conjunction with what we have looked at already, and the other marks that we shall mention later.

Plotting the chronology of the subject's life and assessing whether events have already happened or when they might do so, involves knowing where the lines begin. Horizontal lines should always be read from the thumb side of the hand, and vertical ones from the wrist. Flexibility is the keyword. Remember that in palmistry as in all things concerned with divination nothing is written in stone.

It is impossible to be precise as to where a line starts and where it stops. Lines differ from hand to hand. Some may be stronger in one subject than in another; some may by straight or straighter while others have pronounced curves; some will start at the wrist, others up

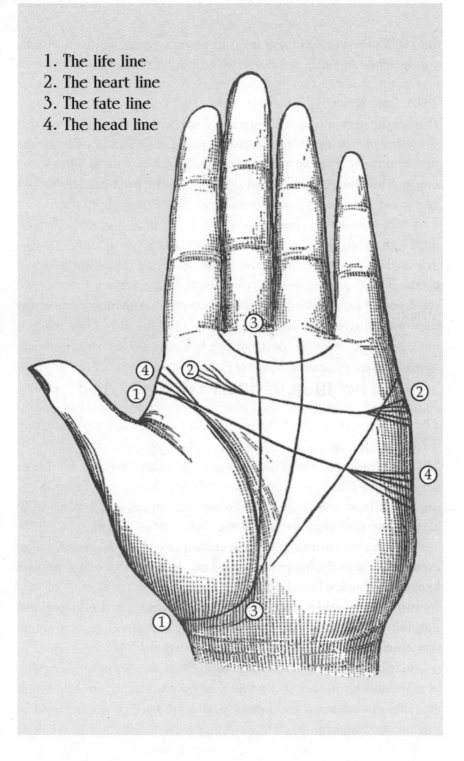

1. The life line
2. The heart line
3. The fate line
4. The head line

from it. The line of one hand may stop at one particular mound while the same line on another subject's hand runs through it.

The life line

This is the line that curves downwards from close to the thumb towards the wrist. The closer to the thumb it starts, then the less vitality the subject is likely to have whereas the wider the curve the greater the energy. A life line that is less well defined than the head line (see below) points to a person who is driven mentally rather than physically.

Chains in the life line are an indication of delicate health, and small lines rising from it denote versatility and physical activity. Lines that seem to swing out of the main one point to a desire to travel and see the world.

Upward hooks along the line after some unfortunate event has been indicated in the reading, suggest that the sitter has made a tremendous effort to get back on her feet after some sort of setback; otherwise they indicate achievement.

Splits along the line point to huge change, conflict perhaps between domestic and professional life, a new job or relationship perhaps.

The heart line

This is the topmost major line, running horizontally from the side of the hand opposite the thumb. It's the line that reveals relationships, not just romantic ones. If it is almost straight, romance plays little part in the subject's life: he or she views other people in a chilly, rational way. A strongly curved heart line points to the subject who loves being in love and shows it, the sort person who takes the lead in any relationship.

A heart line that curves steeply below the index and middle digits indicates strong sexual desires and passions, not promiscuity, though: that can be shown by a short heart line close to the finger and points to the mound of Saturn (see below). Such a line also denotes practicality in matters of the heart. But a line that ends under the middle finger says that the subject is the sort of person who is in constant need of love and reassurance.

If there are lots of branches off the heart line, the sitter enjoys meeting new people and establishing friendships with them.

The fate line

The line that runs from the wrist and runs upwards towards the mound of Saturn represents career, marriage and children – the practical, central supporting aspects of life. A strong fate line indicates that the subject has settled into life's routines and accepts them happily. If it is not there or is very faint, then the sitter is unsettled and might have to change jobs several times before they make their way in life, and will have to do so with little or no help from the family. But one that begins in the mound of Venus (see below) suggests that the family will interfere, particularly in romantic matters and those relating to the sitter achieving his or her ambitions.

A fate line that almost reaches the middle finger says that the subject will enjoy an active old age. One that begins at the head line suggests that academic effort has played an important part in the subject achieving success in life. One that stops at the heart line is an indication of sexual indiscretion.

An overly thick fate line means a period of anxiety at the time of life indicated by the chronology of the reading.

The head line

The line running between the life and heart lines. If it starts off tied to the life line at the start, slavish obedience to and dependence on other people is indicated. If the two lines have distinct starting points (which is usual) a well-balanced, independent nature is indicated.

A long head line points to a person who thinks before he acts: a short one to someone who is quick-thinking and incisive. If the line doesn't slant at all, the subject is likely to be an unsympathetic person lacking in imagination. A slanting line indicates an imaginative and intuitive person. A line that curves rather than slants indicates lateral thinking.

Receptivity to new people is shown by the presence of lots of outward branches on the head line. If they point towards the mound of Jupiter (see below) leadership qualities are suggested. If they point to Saturn, a hardworking nature is indicated and success in a job that requires research. Artistic achievement is indicated by branches that point towards Apollo, and someone with branches pointing towards the mound of Mercury should look to a career in the communications industry or business world. Downward branches suggest periods of depression, but one that runs to the lunar mound opposite to the thumb can expect success in the arts or humanities.

The triangle and the quadrant

The triangular shape that is often formed by the head, heart and life lines also has a meaning, as does the area between the heart and head lines, which is known as the quadrant.

A wide triangle is an indication of an open person, always willing to take action and with passions that are easily aroused. Meanness of spirit is indicated by a small, cramped triangle.

A wide quadrant is an indication of an impulsive nature that cares little for what the world thinks. But a small quadrant, marked with many lines suggests timidity and fear, someone who is constantly concerned about what people think of them.

The minor lines

Whereas most of us have the major lines engraved in the palms of our hands, many of us will not have all of the lines that follow – and their absence can be as significant as their presence.

The success line

Often called the Line of Apollo, the line that runs vertically from the palm towards the ring finger is the line of fame, fortune and success in that which the subject finds important. If it is not there, the subject believes that success can only come through hard work. If there is a break in it, a period of some sort of struggle is indicated.

The health line

Ideally, the line that on many hands runs up the radial side of the hand, towards the little finger and which is sometimes called the Line of Mercury should not be present, for it indicates an overdeveloped concern for health. One that starts close to the mound of Venus (see below) suggests bad digestion and a long health line on a very lined hand says that worry could cause ulcers.

The Mars line
Running inside the life line, this is an indication of someone who has vitality with a capital 'V'.

The via lascivia
A horizontal line that runs across the mound of the Moon (see below) can indicate that the subject suffers from allergies or that an addiction of some sort is causing problems.

The girdle of Venus
If it is there at all, seen as a semicircle above the heart line and covering the mounds of Saturn and Apollo (see below), it says that the subject is a person of an unusually sensitive nature.

Travel lines
Running horizontally from the outer side of the hand, below the little finger and lying across the mound of the Moon (see below) in the lower left corner and on the lower Mars mound (see below) these little lines indicate important journeys. And the stronger and longer they are, the more important is the journey.

Bracelets
These are the horizontal lines between the wrist and the palm. Three of them indicate a long life. If the top one curves and pushes up towards the palm, it could mean that infertility is a problem.

The bow of intuition
A very unusual line found opposite the thumb, starting at the mound of the Moon (see below) and curving up towards the mound of Mercury (see below), this is an indication of intuition and prophetic ability.

The ring of Saturn

Another rare line, seen as a small arc below the middle finger, indicating a reclusive nature and tendencies towards miserliness.

The ring of Solomon

People who are well respected for their common sense often have this line, which runs round the base of the index finger, skirting the mound of Jupiter (see below).

The mounds

The raised pads on the hands are called 'mounds' or 'mounts' and vary in size and the degree to which they are pronounced. They speak of the subject's character. Running widdershins from the base of the thumb, the mounds are as follows:

The mound of Venus

Found at the base of the thumb, it is to do with harmony and love. Broad and well-developed, it suggests a strong sex life and a love of all that is sensual, but also a deep love of the family. Sitting high and soft to the touch it is an indication of excitability and fickleness. If it is depressed or flat, then the subject may by indolent and careless, but before rushing to criticize, this could be caused by ill health.

The mound of Neptune

Sitting at the base of the palm, in the middle of the hand, the mound of Neptune is often not prominent, but when it is so and it is well developed, then the subject is probably a person of some charisma.

The mound of the Moon

At the bottom of the ulna side of the hand, the mound of the Moon is related to travel and to the unconscious. If it is very pronounced, it suggests a person of vivid imagination but introspective nature, with a tendency to mendacity. Sensitivity and a perceptive nature are indicated by a normal-sized Moon mound, while those who have a flat one are probably dull and unimaginative, and unstable people with a frosty nature.

Mars lower

Found on the outside edge of the hand above the mound of the Moon, this represents motivation. If it is large, though, there is a tendency towards violence and argument, while a small one may say that the subject is something of a coward. A normal Mars lower suggests courage, someone who will pick up the gauntlet and fight for a cause he believes in.

The mound of Mercury

Positioned at the base of the little finger, this is the mound of self-expression, of travel and of business abilities. A large one suggests a good sense of humour and a warm, receptive nature. Powers of persuasion, subtlety and quick-thinking are indicated by a normal-size one. But if it is flat, then the subject could well be a bit of a dull loner, shy perhaps or just lazy.

The mound of Apollo or the Sun

Situated at the base of the ring finger, this has to do with success, charm and creativity. High-achievers in the media, on stage and in sport, often have pronounced mounds of Apollo, but they can be prone to hedonism, extravagance and pretentiousness. An undeveloped one indicates a person who is dull, whose life is aimless and has no interest in culture whatsoever.

The mound of Saturn

Sitting at the base of the middle finger, this mound if it is over-prominent suggests someone who is gloomy bordering on being reclusive, so intent is he on keeping his head down and earning money. If it is flat or undeveloped, the person is your ordinary man in the street. If the mound merges with Jupiter (see below) it implies someone who is ambitious and serious. And if it merges with the mound of Apollo (see above) then the subject could well be passionate about the arts.

The mound of Jupiter

This sits at the base of the index finger. Representing how willpower can be used to achieve ambition, this mound, if well-rounded, suggests that its owner is confident that he will succeed. People with large Jupiters like everything to be just so, but they can be generous. If the mound is especially high, then arrogance is a word that is probably associated with the subject. A flat, undeveloped Jupiter is a sign of laziness and selfishness and a dislike of authority.

Mars upper

In the crease of the thumb, a large Mars upper is a sign of bad temper and cruelty, and a sharp, sarcastic tongue. Moral courage is indicated by a normal Mars upper and cowardliness by a flat one.

The plain of Mars

Not a mound, obviously, the plain of Mars is in the hollow in the centre of the palm. If the lines around it are distinct and unbroken, the subject probably enjoys good health and prosperity and can look forward to a long life. Optimism is indicated by a flat plain, but should it be hollow, then in all likelihood the subject lacks both drive and ambition.

Minor marks

As well as using the lines and mounds, diviners can get information from the small marks that many of us carry in the palms of our hands.

Ascending lines

Branching upwards from the main lines of the hand, these indicate extra energy, and if they continue onwards towards one of the mounds, that mound indicates the realm in which that energy is directed.

Crosses

Crosses are not a good sign, as they draw out negative aspects of the line on which they are found, although the less distinct the cross is, the less powerful the draw will be. A cross on the mound of Apollo indicates business or financial disappointment whereas one on the mound of Mercury signifies a dishonest personality.

Relationships will suffer if there is a cross on Venus. A cross on the mound of the Moon suggests someone prone to self-delusion. But worse of all is a cross that is seen on the mound of Saturn, for it signifies that ambitions will be particularly hard to achieve.

Descending lines
Just as an ascending line indicates an energy surge, so descending ones point to there being less energy being directed towards the areas governed by the line from which they fork.

Forked lines
On any of the major lines, forks indicate diversity related to that particular line. Forks on the life line may mean a change in direction at the time indicated by where the fork is. Love affairs or perhaps a change in where the affections lie can be suggested by forks in the heart line. A fork at the end of the fate line points to a successful career bringing fame and fortune. And a fork at the end of the head line is a sign that the subject is a good businessman.

Grilles
Often found on the mounts of the hand, these little noughts and crosses boards denote obstacles ahead in whatever the mound is associated with. Thus, a grille on Venus suggests greedy lust.

Islands
Uneven circles on lines and mounds indicate weakness, listlessness and unwelcome change but changes that could lead to better things – eventually. On the life line for example, islands close to the start mean troubled teenage years. On the heart line, they can signify problems with hearing or sight.

Stars

Something spectacular is in the air when there are stars on the mounds of the hand. On Jupiter (at the base of the index finger) it indicates a good marriage that will enhance career prospects with a consequent boost to finances. On Saturn (base of the middle finger), it suggests that the subject's special talents will bring fame and fortune. On Apollo (base of the ring finger), a star might indicate a major win of some kind or an artistic triumph, whereas a great step forward in knowledge is indicated by a star on Mercury (base of the little finger).

6

ASTROLOGY

Your life, *all* life, on planet Earth: people, animals and plants, depend on the creative force of the Sun's light and warmth for survival. Astrology was born when ancient humans worshipped the Sun for its lifegiving properties. With no knowledge of cosmology, the changing position of the Sun, phases of the Moon, and colour and brightness of the planets and stars were thought to be omens or messages from the gods.

People took the changing patterns in the sky to mirror life on Earth. The timing of events such as: births, deaths, wars and good fortune, were attributed to what was happening in the skies at the time. This celestial search for meaning evolved through many different forms of astrology, all of which reflect the belief that we're all part of one cosmically, interconnected reality.

What are Sun signs?

Your Sun sign is also known as your star sign or horoscope sign: Aries, Taurus, Gemini and so on. It is the sign of the zodiac that the Sun was passing through when you were born. As the Sun is the creator of all life, in astrology the Sun symbolises your core personality traits, your identity – the parts of yourself that you shine out to the rest of the world. Understanding your Sun sign can give you a great deal of insight into what makes you tick and in this book we'll focus on the Sun's influence on your personality, relationships, work, and your well-being.

Does a 13th zodiac sign exist?

In a nutshell, no, because astrology is not astronomy. Every year you'll see stories in the media about the existence of a 13th sign. The argument being that because of the Earth's tilt/wobble its position has changed from that of 3,000 years ago when the signs were first allocated, and the Sun now appears to pass through 13 signs, including the constellation of Ophiuchus. However, astrology focuses on the path of the Sun as it moves along the ecliptic – 12 zones which have the have the same names as constellations, but they are not the same as the actual constellations. There are more than many constellations that border the ecliptic, but Western astrology has only ever used 12.

Cusp dates

The exact time of the Sun's entry into each of the 12 zodiac signs varies every year, making it impossible to list them all. Each zodiac sign is divided into 30 degrees and If you were born a day either side of the dates shown for your Sun sign, you were born on the 'cusp' – the dates where the Sun was transiting from the end degrees of one sign to the start degrees of the next. The Sun cannot be in two zodiac signs at once. People born on the cusp are thought to carry personality traits of the sign the sun has just left – or is about to enter. To know once and for all what your Sun sign is, you can check with an online ephemeris, such as the one available at www.astro.com which shows the exact moment the Sun moved into each zodiac sign.

ARIES (March 21– April 20)

Personality

You are a passionate Fire sign ruled by action-oriented, take-no-prisoners, Mars. Fire Sun signs are usually forthright, energetic and creative with an unrivalled lust for life. As the first sign of the zodiac, you are a natural leader, a pioneering go-getter who lets nothing get in your way. You like to be first and you play to win. You accomplish your goals fast, fearlessly and furiously, and, yes, you may run out of steam a little towards the end of more complicated projects.

Natural enthusiasm

You prefer taking action rather than talking or thinking, and the more challenging a problem the higher its value seems to you. Your reactions are lightning fast, and you instinctively understand how to make things happen. This can make you a little impatient with more considerate types who like to weigh up pros and cons. Your natural assertiveness fires you up to get moving without delay – why would anyone want to waste time discussing the details? You have stuff to do and there's fun to be had!

Spontaneous spender

Cash comes in as fast as it goes out in your world. If you're living in the fast lane you need your money to be there for the spending. Saving is an alien concept because, for you, money in the bank is just an adventure waiting to happen. You're an impulsive spender and if you see something that makes you happy right now, why would you deny yourself? You're the splurge master, spending everything on a fabulous weekend then living on breakfast cereal for the rest of the month.

Fast and furious

You're a very energetic, physical person, which has probably taken its toll on your joints over the years. Your daring antics in your younger years will have a left more than their fair share of scrapes and bruises, but you wear your battle scars proudly. As far as you're concerned, the aim is not to get to the end in perfect condition, the plan is to have lived life as fully and intensely as possible. You prefer to charge in, all guns blazing, do your thing and leave, which is great for dramatic effect, but not so impressive for tasks that require patience and stamina – or are in any way boring! Paperwork, household chores and other necessary but dull activities tend to get left until they threaten to bury you completely.

Brave and uncomplicated

Your courage is legendary and that applies to matters of the heart as well as your physical prowess. You're not frightened to speak out about how you feel and because you're more inclined to extrovert tendencies, you usually find it quite cathartic to express your emotions freely. You accept your feelings readily without prejudice or analysis – you feel what you feel – and that's all there is to it! As a Mars-ruled individual, anger can sometimes boil up to the surface and you're no stranger to a good old-fashioned tantrum. But thanks to your emotional openness, your frustration tends to be explosive, short-lived and quickly forgotten. But explain that to the mild-mannered Piscean whose hair stood on end when you scolded them for not holding the elevator!

Where others fear to speak, you say exactly what's on your mind. You may have a reputation for being a little tactless or abrupt, but you're also admired for your wonderfully outspoken nature. You don't usually set out to intentionally offend anyone, but if you do say something out of turn, you'll not dwell on the consequences too much. More inward-looking Sun signs might gasp in awe at the apparent ease with which you brush off misunderstandings, but you don't place too much importance on chit-chat. You say what most people are thinking, and secretly wish that everyone else would do the same. The world would certainly be a less complicated place if everyone were an Aries!

Honesty is everything

Handling other people's frustration and anger is certainly a life lesson you'll encounter – or will have now mastered. But you're hurt to the core if you discover you've been lied to. In a way you'd rather people just got plain angry or punched you, because then you'd know what you were dealing with. Honesty is your superpower, so to have the lack of it in others used against you can leave you feeling bewildered. Luckily though, you're not usually a brooder, and recover relatively quickly from any setbacks.

Love and relationships

You love with a child-like, uncomplicated joy. You don't have the patience for mind games and rarely waste time on somebody who cannot return your affections. You're open and honest about your feelings and not subtle, which can be a little unnerving! But your uncomplicated approach makes you a refreshing, exciting person to be in love with. You can be a bit bossy at times, but your partner doesn't see this at first because they're so caught up in your ardent, blinding affection. You need a strong other half who can match your energy and who won't be afraid of a challenge.

Fall in love fast

You will have had more than your fair share of experiences of love at first sight, after all, you are the first sign of the zodiac and first impressions mean a great deal to you. You fall hard and fast with a burning desire and you're usually the one who initiates contact. You're not backwards in coming forwards and have a knack for knowing how to impress the person you have your heart set on. As you're not scared to approach people you like, you may have many love relationships in your life before settling on someone special. You have complete faith in yourself, but you take a while to feel that sure about anyone else.

As an energetic Fire sign your sex appeal is obvious, though the intense heat can cool quickly if your lover has a lazy streak or seems to be a bit of a pushover. When you decide you really care about someone, you call off the attack dogs, and your chosen person will discover a very romantic soul.

Independent lover

Even in your closest relationships you're an independent free spirit so sharing your life with someone else can feel a little daunting. Cooking for another can feel like a big deal at first – never mind having to share your living space and time. But if your mate understands and is willing for you to take charge, there won't be too many shouting matches. Though if your partner begins to get too clingy you may have to have an adult conversation.

You hate feeling vulnerable; only a few carefully chosen people ever really get to see the trusting little child in you. But when you feel safe and loved, you let your guard down completely. Your confidence in others' love is hard won, so if you feel taken for granted or disappointed in your partner, it can be devastating. A little naively sometimes, you can't imagine why your lover would be anything but honest and open with you at all times – manipulation just isn't your style.

If someone does break your heart, your grief is real and raw but, because you are able to express yourself so sincerely, you are able to process your emotions more quickly than the other zodiac signs. Phew!

Fight to find the one
Ultimately, you are a fighter and you won't give up on love because you know you deserve it, and your self-belief demands it. You may experience your fair share of romances and break-ups but that's because you're a tougher cookie than most – the Universe knows you can handle it. You may have something of an epic frog-kissing journey to complete before finding your prince or princess, but where's the challenge in finding your true love straight away? You're not one to dwell on past hurts, and eventually see them as milestones on the road as you battle your way to victory in love.

Most compatible love signs
Aries - you love a challenge and only another Aries can handle your lava-hot passion without getting burned.
Leo - you're both enthusiastic and energetic. Leos need to be admired which you're happy to do, as long as they don't mind you bossing them around.
Libra - you're not intimidated by anyone, but there's something mysterious and magnetically appealing about your opposite sign of Libra.

Least compatible love signs

Virgo - won't make love until the house is tidy and they've watched the news.

Taurus - dislikes being rushed and don't like being uncomfortable, which rules out your spontaneous desire to make love on the washing machine.

Cancer - you just plain scare Cancer, who need to feel safe, secure and well understood before anyone is allowed to get close. You don't have time for that!

Work and Career

You love to lead, and you play to win – skills that can make you a legendary boss, and ultimately that's where you're heading! But to get the top banana position you also need to master a few workplace habits and skills. You tend to throw yourself into the deep end, or enthusiastically plunge into new projects without wasting time, which is all very commendable and your boss will appreciate your energy. But a little more preparation will go a long way to help when you get stuck, or bored.

Sharing with others

Let other colleagues know you're available and willing to contribute. Nobody likes someone that pushes in and takes all the glory for themselves. Share your success and include your colleagues in your thinking. Then when you do bump into an obstacle or have to deal with a difficult person, you won't be doing it all on your own.

Ram your way to the top

Your eagerness and boundless energy are admirable and will catch your boss's eye and keep you fresh in their mind. Not everyone is as keen as you are to take on difficult challenges at work, and your innovative ideas will prove popular. You're never stuck for an answer and are often the one to kick off brainstorming sessions.

When your employers trust that you will take on other people's opinions without argument, or can take criticism without stapling their tie to the desk, you'll be worth your weight in gold to any

167

organisation. And when you do get to the top, which is inevitable, you can be the one calling the shots – and everything will fall into its natural astrological order.

Most compatible colleagues

Sagittarius - genial, creative and always full of good ideas – they make you look good.

Taurus - you need Taurus – they're easy to boss around, reliable, and thorough – all the things you're not!

Gemini - you're not hot on details but get on a Gemini's good side and they'll type, talk, look as though they're listening, organise the Christmas party and make tea all at the same time.

Least compatible colleagues

Capricorn - they want to be the boss too, but they're sneakier, or possibly even cleverer about it than you – and you're not keen on that.

Pisces - dreamy Pisces just doesn't have enough urgency about them for you to believe they're getting any work done.

Aries - serious competition here and you really admire their style, but there's no room at the top two alpha Rams!

Ideal Aries Careers

Lion tamer
Firefighter
Ambulance driver
Demolition expert
Professional athlete
Surgeon
First Aid responder
Police officer
Soldier

Well-being

The creative power of the Sun has bestowed you with a robust constitution and athletic abilities. You excel at games and sport and enjoy setting yourself goals and smashing through your targets. You're usually a fast mover but are more of a sprinter than a long-distance runner. Ruled by energetic Mars, you put everything into your efforts but run out of patience if things get too samey. Just changing your daily commute, or the grocery store run, can give you a bit of a lift.

Favourite activities

Boxing, trampolining, hot yoga and running would all be excellent activities for your boisterous sign. You're no couch potato and need to keep yourself busy. Netflix every night would have you, quite literally, climbing the walls (another great activity for you).

You need space around you and plenty of fresh air – and you're not fussed if the weather's bad. Exercising in snow, wind and rain just adds to the challenge for you. You're not usually a team player, preferring the freedom of going it alone, but it's different if we're talking about sport. You excel at any physically demanding team sports and are usually a key player.

Most other zodiac signs just can't match you on physical prowess, and eventually even you can't sustain your cheetah-like pace indefinitely. Because you use up so much energy, it's super-important that you match the energy out with energy back in and get plenty of sleep.

Food and drink

You have a very healthy appetite and burn calories fast. As a Fire sign you enjoy hot, spicy food and are not a particularly fussy eater. Fast food works for you – as long as you balance it up with enough lively activity. If you could, you'd eat out at a different place every day. You don't always have the patience to cook and the thought of sampling new cuisines is too tempting to miss out on. You're more of a street food fan than a leisurely candlelit dinner person, and you prefer to grab and go and have a soft spot for carveries and buffets.

Red meat, hot peppers and curries are Aries foods and you have a penchant for energy drinks. You're not moved by bland tastes – the stronger the better you like it, but go easy on the caffeine and the coffee. You, more than most, need to switch off before going to bed.

TAURUS (April 21 – May 21)

Personality

You are a strong, silent, patient, rock of a person – the metaphorical foundations on which the rest of the zodiac signs are built. As the second sign, you take what Aries initiated, and you create something tangible, beautiful and enduring.

You are solid, trustworthy and unchanging, which can sound a little *too* sensible, but without your strength and dependability, everything else collapses. The salt of the earth, you work towards your goals slowly with determination.

Patience is your superpower. When you know something, somewhere or someone is right for you, you'll accept that it may take a long time to get there. But you know with some certainty that you will. You're not in a rush; you're suspicious of anything that's quickly won, believing the best things in life should be earned.

It's this intractable stubbornness that's so frustrating for the bubblier, quicker-moving zodiac signs hoping you might be a little more flexible.

When your mind is made up, you will not undo it, and if you suspect others of attempting to manipulate you, or they get pushy, you'll simply and calmly stop where you are and will not be moved.

Serene or raging Bull?

Taurus is ruled by delightful Venus, bestowing you with ample good looks and an easy charm. Even skinny Taurus have a solidness to their physiques, and they usually have well-defined eyes and curly hair. Exuding an inner confidence that can be quite irresistible, you long for a partner and will wait patiently for the perfect person. You don't usually choose to waste energy on chasing love – you attract it!

You conserve your physical and emotional energy, which, on the surface may look like nothing ever bothers you. This can occasionally prove irresistible to some, who will amuse themselves by attempting to provoke a reaction in you. But you tend to carry on regardless, in your good-natured, peaceful way.

This often makes people, wrongly, think that you are an emotionless person or are not moved by others' trials and tribulations. Earth signs can get very emotional indeed, it just takes you longer to get there. You try not to be too pulled around by your feelings so that when you really *need* to, you can wield your emotional energy to awesome effect.

When Bulls charge, they lose it, sometimes you might not even remember what happened. You see red and you *become* anger. This can be pretty devastating for the outwardly serene Bull. And it can take you a long time to recover.

All that emotion has to come out somewhere, which is also, incidentally, one of the reasons Taurus makes for a passionate lover. You will move mountains for the people you love. That story you read where a mother had to lift a truck to get to her child – she was almost certainly Taurus.

Honest and hard working

You are a thorough and dedicated worker and you like to do things properly. If you have been pressured to take shortcuts in the past, you probably had a bad experience and won't get caught out again. People trust you to do a proper, honest job and you repay in kind whether you're a bus driver, sculptor, joiner, scaffolder or bank manager.

Taurus has a natural affinity with money, and a knack for accumulating plenty of it. You may own more than one business and your enduring personality gives you the perseverance and ambition to keep going even when times are hard. You trust that eventually you'll make it work.

You're not a workaholic Saturn-ruled Capricorn type who values work over leisure. Venus definitely has something to say about that. You work for money to buy you lots of lovely stuff! And you know how to enjoy a bit of down time. You know how to draw a defining line between work and relaxation.

Home comforts

You adore home comforts. What's the point of working hard for money if you don't have a wardrobe full of exquisite clothes or gorgeous jewellery? You deeply appreciate good food, and you're in your element in any upmarket restaurant. You don't spend much on nightlife, as you prefer quieter, more intimate scenes, and a bit of space around you. Your home is your castle, where you feel most content. An evening spent in your fluffy onesie, surrounded by your family on a plumped-up sofa with a home-cooked meal will never not be appealing. But you even look comfortable on a snatched hour's lunchtime in a busy office. Some Air or Fire signs will be flapping about talking about all there is to do, and your seeming lack of urgency can get on their goat. But your boss and your colleagues, who've known you forever, understand that you're actually one of their best workers. You just take it in your stride and make it look easy.

Love and relationships

Your easy-going nature, down-to-earth sense of humour and Venusian good looks, draw people to you. You don't fall in love easily, but when you do it's usually a life-long commitment as you are a faithful, loyal and devoted partner.

You're a great catch and bring a wealth of treasures to the relationship table, but you require your potential partner to tick quite a few boxes before you return their affections.

You have excellent taste and expect any suitors to be acquainted with the finer things in life. A traditionalist at heart, you respect the tried and tested, more conventional route to romance. You like being wined and dined. Candlelit dinners, flowers, couples' massages and cocktails at sunset all bring a rosy glow to your heart. But the person who is going to make the best impression also has to look, smell and sound good. You're a sensual creature and a person's voice can be a dealbreaker for you – a melodious timbre in a sexy voice will have you weak at the knees. Good cooks definitely have a head start in the competition to catch your eye, as do bankers, jewellers, estate agents and CEOs.

Charming and attractive

Venus, your ruling planet, blessed you with a dollop of loveable charm and serenity, so you won't have to work too hard to attract a suitable other half. When you sense someone is attracted to you, you'll play it safe and slow to begin with, choosing a steady pace that you feel comfortable with. Unless you have plenty of Fire and Air planets in your birth chart, you're not usually a spontaneous or overly-reactive person, which might make it harder for potential mates to know if you are interested at all.

You don't give away your heart easily, or indulge in passionate affairs, but when you've made up your mind about love, you rarely let go. It may take you a long time to get excited about someone, but when you're sure it's a serious romance, you are one of the most passionate lovers in the zodiac – even giving sexy, intense Scorpio a run for their money!

Money matters

You need to feel secure to feel safe, so commitment, whether that's discussing marriage, buying a house together or having a family, relaxes you, and makes you believe your partner is ready to settle down in the same way you are. You work hard for your rewards and are happy to share the spoils with the right person.

Taurus is a money-oriented sign, associated with the second house of the zodiac connected with earnings and possessions. And, rightly or wrongly, you often associate money with self-worth. That's why a joint bank account, with money coming in from both sides, is usually part of your romantic agreements. A healthy bank balance makes you feel secure and valued so choosing someone whose financial intentions are similar to yours is imperative.

Once you're in a committed and secure loving relationship, you're a happy Bull. You shower your chosen one with affection and like to spend much of your time in their company, but this can be a little stifling for more freedom-loving partners. You like to have your loved ones close at hand, where you can see, touch and hear them.

Passionately possessive

It's only natural for the zodiac sign connected with money and possessions to be a little bit clingy with the most important thing in their lives. Once you are comfortable with someone, it's terribly hard to let go. So, when your other half gives you cause to feel insecure, or you fear they're spending more time with other people (or even the dog!) you can become jealous.

A Bull's jealousy is not subtle. You're not used to being rocked by your emotions – anyone who's seen you angry will testify to that! Strong feelings can cause extremes of behaviour in you. When upset you're no stranger to taking a passive-aggressive silent stance and you may even attempt to control your partner.

It will take a few foot massages, expensive chocolates and declarations of absolute devotion, but when the dust settles and you feel reassured, your serenity and your faith in your partner, will be restored.

Most compatible love signs
Capricorn - stable, traditional and sensible, you're both hard workers and have a mutual financial understanding.
Cancer - this protective sign makes you feel safe and well-looked after – and they're usually excellent cooks!
Scorpio - you're attracted to Scorpio's calm exterior and delighted by their secretly passionate interior.

Least compatible love signs
Sagittarius - might need a makeover, shave, new clothes, car and a home before being considered.
Gemini - you want absolute sincerity in a lover. To you Gemini is all chat and no substance.
Aquarius - you need a sensual, passionate lover. Aquarians just aren't.

Work and career
You're one of the most hardworking signs of the zodiac. If you make promises, they'll be delivered. You're not necessarily the speediest but you take pride in your work. Not a huge fan of change, Taurus is the sign most likely to have been in the same job for the longest time. Familiarity makes you feel more at ease. You've probably had the same office chair for years or drunk from the same broken mug.

Safe pair of hands

If you're at the helm, you run a steady ship where everyone knows the rules. You don't tolerate shoddy workmanship and you don't cut corners. Employees need to prove their skills and earn your trust before you feel they're ready to take on added responsibility. As a reliable Earth sign, your workers know you're a safe pair of hands who is brilliant in a crisis. Once you trust someone you work with, you are extremely loyal and move mountains to help them if you feel they've been unfairly treated.

Artistic talents

You find methodical and even repetitive work rather comforting. But that doesn't mean you're not creative. Ruled by artistic Venus, you're an extremely patient and artistic soul who can spend weeks perfecting a painting, working on a sculpture or composing a concerto. You're a comfort-loving creature who appreciates good workmanship and would make an excellent luxury clothes designer or furniture maker. You're also known for having the loveliest singing voice in the zodiac.

Most compatible colleagues

Capricorn - you understand this fellow Earth sign's stoical approach and respect that they didn't take any shortcuts to get where they are.
Aries - you're thorough, but you're not fast – you need Aries to help you get out the starting blocks, then you'll take it from there.
Pisces - you're both artistic but Pisces have no stamina, so you're happy to plunder their imagination in return for some donkeywork.

Least compatible colleagues

Gemini - they talk the talk but, as far as you're concerned, they don't walk the talk.
Leo - the quality of your work usually outshines Leo, but you wouldn't know it from all the attention seeking and social media sharing they do about theirs.
Libra - you're at your best when you know exactly what is required of you. Libra can't even decide which cookies to buy for the coffee break!

Ideal Taurus Careers
Banker
Farmer
Builder
Singer
Gardener
Restaurant owner
Wine producer
Musician
Sculptor
Interior designer

Well-being

Robust, with a strong physique, you are usually in rude health. You're not terribly athletic but you do have plenty of stamina often brought on by sheer, dogged determination. When, and if, you do take up regular exercise, you prefer a predictable routine to fit into your well-ordered lifestyle. You like having a fitness buddy but if they can't stick to the arranged times, you'll find someone who can.

A true Taurus is a slow, purposeful mover who has one speed – their own. You hate to be rushed into anything – even if food is on the agenda! If you're being harassed to get on with something, you'll simply stop in your tracks and close down. You win at life through force of will. You may be weathered, battered and bruised, but you'll make it to the finish line. Other zodiac signs just can't get anywhere near your pain threshold or match you on stubbornness.

Food and drink
No sign of the zodiac is as enamoured with food as you. For Taurus food is an all-consuming experience. Food takes you to another world. Earth signs are attracted to tangible things and eating involves all your senses – it's got to look as good as it tastes. But, of course, your passion for food can lead to overindulgence, which can cause weight gain. You're lucky that you have a sturdiness that doesn't look out of place on a person who's a few pounds overweight – you can definitely carry

it off. And, traditionally, as a Venus-ruled sign, you're usually pretty easy on the eye, which can all disguise an extra bit of padding!

Love to lounge

Sensual with exquisite taste in clothes, you spend good money on leisurewear. You're often the most stylish person at the gym or yoga class, wearing expensive soft, natural fabrics. You're not quite as enamoured with exercise though. Getting sweaty, out of breath and uncomfortable with unkempt hair is all a bit too uncomfortable for you.

The gym might not be your natural home but enjoying being outside in the fresh air is a different story. You are a hardy walker, most at peace in the bucolic countryside with a lazy picnic on the agenda.

Taurus have turned lounging into an artform. Soft deep chairs, flattering lighting, candles and soft music are basics in your home. Your bed will be unusually luxurious with money splurged on sumptuous fabric.

GEMINI (22 May – 21 June)

Personality

You are the most versatile sign of the zodiac. Intelligent, adaptable and effervescent, you're the cleverest – and most easily bored – kid in town. You're the third sign, ruled by inquisitive Mercury, the communications planet and you know *something* about everything, but you're not much of a specialist. Once you get your mind around something new, you're already half-thinking about what's around the corner. Your puppy-like mental enthusiasm keeps you bright, boisterous and burning for more.

Whether it's astrophysics or pottery, you have an unrelenting thirst for knowledge and new experiences. This butterfly mentality means you can sometimes struggle with the Earthier qualities of stability, commitment and determination. You live so much in your mind that you can forget to return messages, turn up late for important events and sometimes just stop halfway through sentences, chasing your own train of thought down a plughole. You can't imagine why anyone would mind that you missed the boat for a dinner date or would think it rude that you forgot to take your friend to a sports game. Maybe you were side-tracked by a phone conversation or suddenly had to understand how mathematical equations work... surely that's more important than being bang on time for your sister's wedding?

Intellectual and detached

Your emotional reactions are often as mysterious to you as they are to others. It's not that you don't have feelings, of course you do. It's just that you trust in more logical and intellectual pursuits. Strong emotion can feel disconcerting to you, and to lessen its pull, you may appear sunny and bubbly on the outside, even if beneath the surface you're in a black mood.

Because you prefer learning about things, rather than experiencing them, you often fool the people closest to you (and probably therapists everywhere) into thinking you are more in touch with the source of your emotional turmoil than you actually are.

You can talk about how angry, jealous or broken-hearted you are feeling but being willing to investigate the source of the pain feels a little alien. To block out any unpleasant emotions you'll become even more distracted, busy and fragmented.

None of this means you're not kind or compassionate – the opposite is true. It's your natural ability to see things from all sides that makes you so sensitive to others' points of view. When you connect with someone on a mental level, magic happens. You are truly skilled at understanding how other people's minds work. You're fascinated by what makes them tick and want to comprehend the mechanisms that drives their reasoning and forms their opinions.

Light and dark

It's the disconnect between your emotional and mental nature, and your skill for impersonation, that reflects the dual nature associated with your zodiac symbol, the Gemini Twins. You flit between funny, light and sociable, to dark, indifferent and unfathomable. Your moods are as Airy and changeable as the weather, flitting from serene blue skies one minute to stormy rain clouds the next.

When people closest to you hear others talking about you, they're sometimes stumped that you're all talking about the same person. You adapt and change chameleon-like, blending in and agreeing with the last person you spoke with. Trying to pin a Gemini down to tell you exactly what they think of any one thing is a little like chasing a rainbow. It appears solid from a distance but when you get up close it shifts and changes.

Restless curiosity

Sensing your love of gossip and drawn in by your wicked sense of humour, people find you so disarming that they often overshare. Your flattering attention to detail and ability to mentally empathise lets others feel they can let their guard down. They exchange more information than they had intended, and hope you'll keep schtum.

You have probably learned the hard way to keep your mouth closed. Information and entertainment are your currency and it's hard to resist not passing on some juicy gossip, even if that's with someone you shouldn't! It is quite possible for you to keep things to yourself, but if you're bored or restless the temptation may be just too strong. And a bored Gemini is dangerous.

When boredom takes hold, your curiosity can bring out the 'dark twin' who can be provocative and manipulate facts for your own enjoyment. What you see as harmless banter might actually be unkind, wildly exaggerated or even blatantly untrue. This fickle behaviour can earn you a reputation as being superficial.

On the other hand, a focussed Gemini is a genius at work. When you're mentally engaged, you'll get through your work twice as fast as everyone else and the results will be intelligent, thoughtful and entertaining.

Love and relationships

You're one of the friendliest signs of the zodiac and you fall a little bit in love with anyone and everyone when you first get to know them. You're drawn to new people and situations in a way no other zodiac sign is. Where others are shy or even a little fearful of others, your boundaries are quite fluid.

You typically experience a few romances before you settle on one person. And Gemini is the most likely sign of the zodiac to consider an open, or an unconventional, approach to relationships. You may prefer to live in separate houses or even in different countries. You're willing to consider love relationships with people much older, or younger, than you, and long-distance romances can work too, as long as you talk to each other regularly. You're attracted to people who are different to the norm, who are from a different culture or who live an alternative lifestyle. Open-mindedness and a willingness to try something different are Gemini aphrodisiacs. And unless you have Earth or Water signs in your birth chart – you're unlikely to be the possessive or jealous type.

Friendly and fun-loving

For you to fall hard for someone, there has to be something enduringly fascinating about your chosen person. A bright intellect and enthusiasm for life will keep you coming back for more and sharing common interests will help you work towards a shared goal. A nimble dance partner with whom to master complicated steps, will literally keep you on your toes – and any two-person sport such as tennis, squash and snooker will give you both an active focus. Games such as backgammon, Trivial Pursuit and chess keep you challenging each other's mental skills, and if the pair of you can curl up together with a crossword puzzle together, that's certainly a promising sign.

A compatible sense of humour is also essential. You'll feel oddly flat or bored with a lover who takes you too seriously. If your own stories, puns and witty remarks fall short, you might wonder what the point of the relationship is at all. Some light sarcasm and teasing will tickle your mind and keep the atmosphere light and airy, just how you like it.

Above all, you value open communication in your relationships. You love talking – it's your superpower! You need to feel your partner is on the same level and are only truly content when there is constant rapport.

Strange waters

You either say, 'I love you' all the time, to everyone, and everything, or you voice it to a lover occasionally but only when you really, truly mean it. Falling for someone, hook, line and sinker can take you by surprise. You're not wholly comfortable being so dependent on another person's affection. Because you're a little detached from your own feelings, experiencing such forceful emotions toward someone else can be unsettling.

You meet the world around you on an intellectual level, and living in your mind is your safe place. Romantic love brings overwhelming happiness and excitement but it can also provoke tricky feelings like feeling vulnerable or sad when your other half has upset you. Jealousy and possessiveness are deep, strange waters for you – unmanned territory that can't be navigated by brain power or conversation alone.

Overthinking your feelings

You do your best to ignore your more disquieting emotions, but eventually those feelings will need to be experienced, and this disconnect can bring your broodier, moodier Twin to the table.

Analysing and intellectualising your emotions won't make them disappear and experiencing an alien feeling like anger or fear, and not being able to think it away, can be bewildering. It's this dissociation that brings your dual nature to life. When you're unsure what's causing difficult feelings, your mood can quickly change.

Learning that you can be so affected by other people's emotions – and that your own actions have emotional consequences on others, will be your most transformative lesson. To bond with another, you must first bond with yourself – and once you recognise that, your relationships will go from strength to strength.

Most compatible love signs

Aquarius - you both have unusual and sometimes downright eccentric tastes and never tire of each other.

Pisces - you blend into one another seamlessly, not quite knowing where one ends and the other begins.

Leo - you're a glamorous couple – you both enjoy being the centre of attention and you're attracted to Leo's outgoing, open nature.

Least compatible love signs

Scorpio - you're initially attracted to this mysterious zodiac sign, but all that brooding intensity terrifies you a little.

Gemini - you tickle each other mentally and you'll always be friends, but you'll drive each other a little mad in the long term.

Taurus - You're attracted by Taurus' smouldering, sexy aura but Bulls love routine and stability – values you're not that crazy about.

Work and career

As a flexible Air sign, you adapt very easily to new or changing situations. You're a quick, logical decision maker who instinctively knows what to do before the Earth and Water signs have had a chance to finish their first cup of coffee. Your verbal dexterity and dazzling patter make you a gifted salesperson, convincing people they need things they're not even interested in. Your knack for understanding how other people tick is well suited to working in advertising, television, public relations and all communications industries.

Trying something different

You're not interested in traditional ways of doing things, or how things may always have been done in the past. You're rather brilliant at translating complex ideas into workable plans of action. A happy employee, as long as you're always engaged, you'll likely be the chattiest person in the workplace. You enjoy interacting in large teams with a varied bunch of people. Talking on the phone is second nature, and jobs that entail constant interaction with people would also work out peachily.

Unpredictable and mischievous

If you become bored at work, you'll be easily distracted and prone to mischief. Your 'other twin' will make an appearance and you may become disruptive or provocative just to rock the boat for your own amusement. Your unemployed mind will simply find something else to keep it occupied... gossiping with colleagues, scanning social media, learning the latest dance craze or Googling your colleagues to find salacious gossip, will all fill the void.

Most compatible colleagues

Aries - Fire and Air is a fast and furious team... just persuade a Virgo to clean up the mess afterwards.

Aquarius - you spark off each other mentally for some moments of pure genius and are probably friends outside of work, too.

Cancer - with your intellectual empathy, and their emotional sensitivity, you can sell anything from frozen peas to new shopping centres together.

Least compatible colleagues

Capricorn - these guys are too inflexible and traditional to appreciate your youthful zest and brilliance.

Gemini - you can both talk the talk – but one of you also needs to get some work done.

Libra - Libra likes to weigh things up carefully before making important decisions while you just want to give it a go and see what happens.

Ideal Gemini Careers

Advertising
Writer
Teacher
Translator
Gymnast
Computer programmer
Engineer
DJ
Juggler
Librarian

Well-being

As the zodiac's first Air sign, you need to move about. Air is never still, and you crave plenty of variety to keep you feeling active, positive and content. An unusually speedy walker, you often get to your destination faster than public transport.

Long hikes and planned tours aren't really your cup of tea, as you get a little impatient once you have the gist of things or can see the end point in the distance. By then, you're usually ready to take on the next challenge.

Food and drink

Unless you have some Earth sign placements in your birth chart, eating the same food at the same time is not your bag. You tend to be more of a picker than a heavy meal sort of person. In fact, you can find large plates of food quite off putting. You prefer to eat little and often.

New restaurants, cafes and market stalls are often just as interesting to you as the fare on offer. As food is such a vast subject for you to get your teeth into, you rarely tire reading or hearing about it. Sometimes watching cooking programmes will satisfy your appetite almost as much as preparing the food itself.

You're a 'two starters' type of diner rather than plumping for a large main course.

With a taste for the unusual, it's exotic flavours and new products that intrigue you. If someone offered you a peanut butter and artichoke sandwich, you wouldn't say no. You might not eat the whole thing, but you'll certainly give it a go!

Caffeine can send a restless Gemini into overdrive, so it's best to avoid coffee or energy drinks if you want a decent night's sleep. As you burn so much energy, you will need to keep yourself hydrated with plenty of water, and fruit juices also complement your zippy metabolism.

Light and flexible

Nimble and fast on your feet, you burn more calories than the average person before you've set foot in a gym or added any extra activity to your normal day. You lose interest in repetitive training exercises, but Wii fit and interactive dance or Zoom lessons should be fun or entertaining enough to burn off some physical, and mental, steam. When you do need a workout, you tend to go for intense, short bursts of activity such as spin classes or interval training. What you lack in strength and stamina you make up for in agility and your legendary flexibility can make you a spectacular gymnast.

CANCER (22 June - 22 July)

Personality

Ruled by the Moon, your ever-changing moods reflect the lunar cycles as they wax and wane. In astrology the Moon represents our emotions, instincts and reactions, and with your Sun in the Moon's territory, your feelings are magnified. The Crab is your zodiac symbol, depicting your tough, outer personality – protecting and hiding the softer, more vulnerable, inner you.

You don't need, or want, to be the centre of attention. You know what you're doing, and you're a private person who just wants to be left alone to get on with things. Your kindly, firm, maternal manner, garners trust from the people around you who instinctively understand that you're looking out for them and are happy for you to take control.

You can be a little shy, and even standoffish, with people you don't know, but that's just because you're such a giving person. People need to earn your trust before you reveal what a sensitive soul you are inside. It would drain your mental and emotional energy to invite just anyone under your shell. Over the years the people closest to you appreciate that you take your time to break new ground and they give you a bit more time and space to get used to new people and situations..

You know what you want

When you set your heart or mind on something, you're impressively tenacious. You're not usually impulsive or forthright, preferring to wait and watch before deciding on a course of action. Like a crab under the cover of moonlight, you're too self-conscious to strut your stuff and launch yourself into the middle of the action. When you have your eyes on the prize, you're clever and focussed, but rarely approach your goals directly.

A sidling, undercover advance, keeps you hidden from danger, and then at the last moment, when the coast is clear, you'll raise your pincers, grab your treasure then scuttle back to the safety of your home.

Clinging to the past
Partly because you find it so hard to let go, you have an affinity with old things – and that includes the past. You tend to romanticise or hark back to a better time, probably because it feels safer to lose yourself in memories, than to deal with an uncertain future. A lover of tradition, antiques and history, you attach sentimental value to things that baffle your nearest and dearest: old photographs, cumbersome items given to you by people long departed, or perhaps an attic stuffed with old baby clothes and toys. You still find comfort in these old things and guard them carefully. Ancient love letters, records and even bus tickets that remind you of a special person or period in your life – they all remind you of a time you felt loved and safe. In extreme cases, you no longer see these things as clutter but, often quite unconsciously, as more of an extension of your own protective layer or shell.

Dramatic worrier
Whether you're male or female, the Moon is linked with motherhood and you are a born caregiver. Your instincts are to love, nurture and protect without asking for much in return. You're a tough nut to crack because inside you're the softest, most beautiful soul, sensitive and easily hurt. Once you care, and let people into your enormous heart, you don't quite know how to give them up.

You love nothing better than a bit of catastrophizing because it confirms your fears that everything is about to go terribly wrong. You're the person that brings up that one time when things *did* go badly in the past – and your memory of it is crystal clear – even if you weren't actually there!

When things do go awry for people you love, you're genuinely sympathetic. Their pain and disappointment chimes with your own vulnerabilities, and you're a wonderful listener. Never judgmental or harsh, you don't question much about what happened – someone you love is in trouble, that's enough. You'll offer the coat off your back, a warm, safe place to spend a few nights, and a nourishing meal. It won't even enter your mind that you may be inconvenienced or put you out of pocket for a while. The people you love come first, end of story.

Soft underbelly

Most people are nowhere near as tuned into the world of feeling as you, and would be mortified to think you'd taken offence. They're genuinely confused by your hurt reactions, baffled you could take such a trivial thing to heart. If you're really hurt by someone's behaviour you retreat into your shell, the silent treatment usually gets your message across. But if a loved one has angered you, it's a different story. It happens rarely, but when you take revenge it's usually in secret, quietly executed, and devastating!

Thank goodness you have an excellent sense of humour to take the sting out of the most emotionally tense situations. Laughing reminds you that nothing is ever that bad – even if it feels really intense.

Love and relationships

When you're attracted to someone it scares you a little. Your first instinct is to hide and think it through, which usually means worrying about how things could pan out. After all, it could all go miserably wrong... like that time you were hurt in the past... or when your friend's husband was caught cheating. Your mind spins out before you know any real facts about your sexy stranger.

Training your imagination will probably turn out to be a lifetime's endeavour and you have such a tender heart that romance may be something of a learning process. As you get older and better understand your own and others' requirements in relationships, you'll learn to be more realistic. But you, more than any other zodiac sign, have the emotional capacity and understanding to navigate the human heart.

Protecting your heart

When someone intriguing takes the first steps to get to know you, it can set off your defence mechanisms, and you'll be wary. Secretly you'll be flattered, but you'll worry yourself into a frenzy. And all this happens before you even know if this person is even truly flirting with you. You understand what a big deal giving even a tiny piece of your heart is – because the rest of your heart is usually close behind.

When you've been reassured enough from a potential lover, or have decided to trust him or her anyway, you are one of the most romantic people in the zodiac. You're an imaginative and generous lover and you'll place your partner at the centre of your universe.

Emotional compatibility

When you choose to love somebody, you're all-in. When you let someone inside that crabby shell, there's no half measures. Domestic bliss is your aim and setting up a home and family will be paramount. Whether you're angling for a big house full of children or are happy with a pretty little garden and a budgie, your home set-up is where you feel safe, secure and loved.

You put down roots when you're at home, intending to build a base for life and your partner needs to share that vision. Fire and Air signs may be too independent and adventurous for you to settle down with, or you'll need to make sure you both have a clear understanding of what the other needs. As long as the trust is there, you can be happy with someone who wants space to do their own thing.

Emotional compatibility is the single most important factor in your relationships. Your bond with a lover is so tight that you'll feel it if something isn't right – and will be hurt or confused if they're not sharing every emotion with you. You expect to be able to talk to your other half about everything – and expect the same level of openness from him or her. You make it so easy for others to express themselves that this isn't usually a problem. And when you have a contented, established relationship with a happy home life, you'll love without asking for much in return.

Taking things personally

When your emotional needs are met, you tend to place your partner on a pedestal. You will defend their actions, and sometimes excuse them, even when friends or family might raise an eyebrow.

When you do have a disagreement with your partner things can get heated fast and the insecurity can knock you off balance. Your fight or flight response is strong, and disagreements or misunderstandings can fill you with foreboding. Your beloved may accuse you of being overly dramatic or too needy, and that can wound you. It's difficult for you to remember that all relationships have to navigate a few hurdles from time to time, without causing insurmountable problems.

Even when there's nothing to worry about, your oversensitive nervous system may pick up on others' energies and you'll be tempted to interpret them to suit your own suspicions. This can leave your partner feeling perplexed. It may take you a while for your defences to come down again, but when you do, you'll be back to being one of the most generous and loving souls in the zodiac.

Most compatible love signs

Taurus - you both crave security, loyalty and a healthy bank balance and you'll adore each other's sensual nature, too.

Capricorn - your opposite sign is patient and reassuring and can teach you how to balance home and career.

Scorpio - you understand Scorpios because you are both emotionally driven with cool exteriors – they'll be tolerant of your changeable moods.

Least compatible love signs

Aquarius - you want someone to build a comfortable home with, but Aquarius has plans to join the circus.

Sagittarius - warm-hearted, enthusiastic but tactless, you need someone to be your soulmate, not your puppy.

Libra - they say all the right things, but do they *feel* them?

Work and career

Your ideal work situation involves looking after people to some degree. One-to-one employment on a personal basis such as a healthcare professional, counsellor or beauty therapist fulfils your selfless enjoyment of making other people happy. But your understated, excellent people skills also mean you would excel as a charity CEO, a public relations consultant, or as a politician campaigning for better conditions in your community.

You also love working with food – it's your way of nurturing people and it's not by accident you're known as the best cook in the zodiac.

Care and dedication

You're better with money than most, appreciating its security. You're a saver at heart and even when you're pretty flush by anyone else's standards you're likely to plead poverty. The thought of not being able to pay your rent or mortgage, or risking your home, is one of your biggest anxieties and you're not frightened of taking on jobs that others would turn their noses up at to keep a roof over your head. You'll clean streets, unblock toilets or busk outside the train station in the pouring rain if it brings in enough cash to care for your children. It's this dedication to others that also causes you to be a passionate fundraiser or advocate for people less fortunate than yourself.

You're stealthily ambitious and determined to keep your position for as long as possible. Your people-handling skills and unassuming manner impresses most employers who will appreciate your loyalty and calm manner.

Crabby boss

Behind your shy exterior beats the heart of a leader! As a gentle, but firm, parental figure, you often rise to the top of your profession. Co-workers admire your quiet, strong leadership skills and learn that a little cajoling and kindness from you is sometimes all that's needed to exert authority. You're not a demanding or aggressive boss, preferring to connect with your work buddies on a more personal level.

Most compatible colleagues

Cancer - kindred spirits – you both appreciate how to make and save money and you're both very tactful around each other.

Virgo - you both enjoy helping others and Virgo responds well to your humble leadership style.

Pisces - Pisces likes peace and privacy in their working environment and you both appreciate that not everyone has to shout about their accomplishments.

Least compatible colleagues

Leo - you're good at spotting money-making opportunities and Leo's good at spending it!

Libra - isn't as ambitious as you and sees work as an extension of their social life.

Gemini - great at multitasking – not so good at concentrating on important details.

Ideal Cancer careers

Nurse
Nursery teacher
Social services
Relationship counsellor
Insurance
Gardener
Midwife
Museum worker
Chef
Security guard

Well-being

You're sensitive to the phases of the Moon, which push and pull your emotional states. Your fluctuating feelings are the main gauge of your well-being. When you're feeling happy, safe and secure, you have heaps of energy, a hearty appetite, and all feels well with the world. When your feelings are out of whack, your sensitive digestive system can be the first to feel something's not right.

Sometimes at a full Moon you need to be a little kinder to yourself, as you can be your own worst critic when you're feeling out of sorts emotionally. This state of flux can be reflected in worry or stress in your body. No other sign is as affected by their own positive or negative thoughts, and emotional states, as you. If you are prone to feeling unwell when anxious, the same should be true when you're feeling strong and therefore able to heal yourself.

Food and drink

For better or worse, food is usually your chosen comfort. You tend to eat when you're feeling anxious, bored or excited, and sometimes just because it's delicious and wonderful! You love traditional, old restaurants steeped in history almost as much as you adore a home-cooked roast dinner with friends at home.

Cooking and sampling your delicious meals can see unwanted weight creep up on you. But your talents in the kitchen means you're flexible and willing to experiment, so it shouldn't be too much of a chore to choose lighter or more unusual options.

As a Water sign, drinking plenty of fluids keeps you feeling balanced. A glass of delicious wine or an exciting cocktail will often be chosen as a special treat. If you punish yourself for eating and drinking too much, you can become entrenched in some unhealthy habits, or be subconsciously sending yourself unhelpful messages around food. 'A little bit of what you fancy does you good' would be a healthy motto.

Soothing activities

You dislike feeling uncomfortable, so getting sweaty and breathless isn't your thing – aggressive forms of exercise disturb your equilibrium. Gentler forms of exercise, such as yoga, walking and swimming, all soothe your nerves and coordinate your physical and emotional energies.

Being near water relaxes you almost as much as swimming in it. A walk along a beach or a stroll by a river soothes your water-ruled constitution in a magical manner. You're a sensual person and the gentle rhythm of the waves just feels right on a very primal level.

LEO (23 July - 23 August)

Personality

You are regal, dignified, courageous Leo, ruled by the life-giving creative force of the Sun. And, like the Sun, your place is at the centre of the solar system, where everything revolves around you!

In a birth chart the Sun represents the self, the ego, the personal spark of the divine, which means you need to shine. With your passionate, creative, Fire sign energy, you're full of warmth and positivity – and sparkle with life.

Commanding and authoritative, you can have a slightly condescending manner, but that's usually because you genuinely feel you know what's best for everyone. You were born to lead the pack, to encourage, protect and provide for others – so you need other people to give you a sense of purpose. Your motivation is usually to make other people happy and, yes, you can be a little bit firm in enforcing your rules sometimes. But you know you are strong and brave and that your intentions come from the heart. It's this generosity of spirit that makes you one of the most popular signs of the zodiac.

Love is your reason for living. When you're the centre of attention, or on stage in some way, the applause and validation fill you with rays of joy, which you radiate back out to your admirers like a little Sun.

Creating something wonderful

Powered by the regenerative force of the Sun, most Leo wish to change the world for the better – and what better way than to create something beautiful? You were born with the talent and self-confidence to show off your skills, and you're not shy about displaying your brilliance – you see it as your gift to the Universe. But for all your swagger and bravado, you do need encouragement. Leo has to know that what they're doing is unique and wonderful and that nobody else can offer what they can. Inside every Leo there's a little innocent child, who craves love and reassurance. And when the praise comes you prefer it to be as flattering and dramatic as possible... preferably sung from rooftops or displayed on an aeroplane banner.

kindly bossy-boots

You often find it easier to get others' lives in order, rather than concentrating on your own priorities. This is partly because it's easier for you to focus on what other people need out of a genuine concern for their welfare. But it's also because you're such a naturally extroverted character that doing things for yourself, on your own, just doesn't excite you that much.

Some of your friends and family may label this over-eagerness to help as bossiness. But you'll usually argue that you're just pushing them to be the best they can – and ignore their pleas! The thing is, Leo, you're such a wise and knowledgeable person that others will naturally gravitate toward you for advice anyway.

Essential playtime

It's a Leo myth that you're a 'lazy lion'. You're one the zodiac's most dedicated workers, but once the graft is done, you play, luxuriate and indulge your senses. You're an exuberant partier, with exquisite tastes. Champagne bubble baths, expensive night clubs, the finest wines known to humanity, clothes of spun gold... male or female, you embody the playboy archetype.

You love a lie-in and certainly enjoy being catered for. You will put in extra hours at the office if it means avoiding menial chores if you can help it. No self-respecting true Leo will look you in the eye while pulling hairs from the plughole. You'll happily hire nannies, dog walkers, cleaners, accountants and sometimes chefs to free up your precious time.

Learning to love alone time

The problem with thinking the world revolves around you, is that when there's nobody around to watch you be fabulous, you might as well be invisible. Nothing hurts you more than being ignored; after all, you're doing 'all this' for everyone else's benefit. You're not one for self-contemplation, but that's exactly what you need from time to time because you could do with balancing out your need for external validation with some of your own healthy esteem. You must have time out from others to remember what *you* want.

Take a night off and see what happens, just you, no social media and no communication with the outside world. Find out who you really are, Leo. It won't take long for your creative instinct to kick in and you'll find that making something will give you a purpose, without requiring an audience. Dressmaking, painting, collage and baking are all projects where you can share your creations with the people you love – and they'll really appreciate your generosity.

You don't often let other people see you when you're not 'on show'. You're all for false eyelashes, high fashion, sharp suits and flash cars. Your loved ones will see past your glam-armour, but perhaps you need to be a little kinder to the raw, unshaved, dressing gown and slippers, you, too. Deep down you're actually just a little pussycat asking to be loved.

Love and relationships

As an exuberant, warm, effusive person you don't find it difficult to show your affections. You feel alive when you're attracted to someone new – you'll feel full of possibilities and puppy-like enthusiasm. You're an excellent judge of character and will normally be pretty sure that your intended will at least feel some of the excitement you're experiencing.

You'll be tentative at first and if there's any uncertainty you'll hold back until you're sure you can win his or her heart. The slightest hint of reciprocation will light the touch-paper and then you'll gleefully pounce. You're all in for love. You don't understand why anyone would play mind-games – surely if you're both sure of one another, there's no point in pretending otherwise?

Grand romantic gestures don't get more dramatic than a Leo in love. You take all the conventional love clichés and cover them in gold and glitter. You love like you want to be loved in return – with an adoring, ardent, unquenchable passion. Thinking you can show how much you love someone by showering them with gifts and attention, your other half will be bowled over by your generosity and care – and perhaps a little overwhelmed.

When you put so much of yourself into making your life together a fabulous, romantic adventure, you do expect your partner to reciprocate in kind. The problem here is that few people find it so natural and easy to be as generous with themselves as you. You set the bar so high that it's a lot for your lover to live up to. They might be worried about spending too much money on lavish gifts, or a little timid in expressing so much emotion.

This can be disappointing for Leo, as you crave public shows of affection. If someone loves you, they too should trumpet it from the heavens, empty their bank account and plan oodles of secret romantic trips – because that's how *you* do it – that's how love is done! You can be a hard act to follow for more modest types who show their affections in a quieter, less dramatic way. And you have to learn that love can be deep and passionate without everything being for show.

Mutual enthusiasms

Togetherness is hugely important for you in a relationship. You can accept if your other half has other obligations and responsibilities, as long as your time together is spent doing something interesting. Shared pastimes are vital so finding someone with a matched love for drama and entertainment would be a big plus. Getting excited about the same things, whether that's frequent trips to the movies, attending dance classes or a love of cosplay will fuel your need for fun and togetherness.

Your beloved will hopefully enjoy being part of a fashionable or exciting social scene, because if they're happy to lounge around in an old tracksuit covered in doghair, you may have to rethink how it's going to work.

Partner pride

What other people think of your partner is a big issue. If friends or family disapprove, you'll do your best to win them over by over-emphasising their good points or making them out to be more glamorous or exciting than they actually are – or want to be. This tendency to embellish the more mundane aspects of your life together can make your partner feel that they're not living up to your expectations – or being allowed to be who they are.

You are extremely proud of your partner, and want to show him or her off, and see their behaviour and appearance as inextricably linked to your own personality. So, when your adored chooses to be themselves, happy to spend all day reading or tinkering with their car, you can feel ignored and alone – two emotions you're really uncomfortable with.

You are loving, supportive and generous in your relationships but you probably need to learn that being alone together and making each other happy is more important than the drama you play out for your adoring public.

Most compatible love signs

Libra - what a glamorous, charming pair – you both know how to impress other people and love being the centre of attention.

Sagittarius - You're the two most generous people in the zodiac. You'll have heaps of fun and enjoy emptying your joint bank account together!

Gemini - the sparkling entertainment team is here, and neither of you will get a wink of sleep when the other is around.

Least compatible love signs

Leo - you can get jealous when there's another big cat on the scene, stealing all the limelight.

Scorpio - lots of passion initially, but Scorpio's broody emotions and shady game-playing is too underhand for an upfront Leo.

Capricorn - Goat people are not usually emotionally demonstrative, which will cool your need for praise super-fast.

Work and career

On a deep level you respect that if you are to enjoy the best things in life, you need to work solidly for them. Your perfect job is one where you can shine and be admired, while making oodles of cash. You want to bring people joy and pleasure, and to be heartily rewarded and thanked for your efforts.

Need to shine

As one of the most creative and artistic signs of the zodiac, finding work that's an extension of your self-expression, would be an ideal fit. Whether you are offering gorgeous artwork, cooking wonderful food or crafting unique furniture, you need to be proud of your accomplishments and feel that they enhance other people's lives too.

Centre stage

You excel in any position where the focus is on you. Acting is often described as the perfect job for Leo because it involves performing in the spotlight, receiving applause, and adopting a glamorous public image. The entertainment industry has a magnetic pull for Leo looking for the limelight, and singing, dancing or a career in music will be high on your list.

King of the jungle

Leo takes charge instinctively, so being where the buck stops is where you are most comfortable. Your love of showing people what to do and encouraging them to grow makes you a popular boss. A patient teacher, you want others to appreciate your wisdom and experience, and to show some gratitude for your efforts. In return, you are generous and reward loyalty handsomely. It's champagne all round when you're celebrating success and you thoroughly enjoy watching people bask in the benefits you provide as the leader of the pack.

Most compatible colleagues

Taurus - loyal, consistent and hard-working, Taurus and Leo work towards the same goals – the finer things in life.
Leo - you both work and play well together but you will have to timeshare the spotlight.

Sagittarius - as a team, your vision and creativity is breathtaking but you'll need someone who's more practical on board, too.

Least compatible colleagues

Virgo - these guys think of everything, but they spend too much time agonising over tiny details.

Capricorn - takes work very seriously and never seems to enjoy it. You're no workaholic and your down time is crucial.

Pisces - your upfront, noisy, brash approach alarms Pisces who needs a tranquil quiet space.

Ideal Leo careers

Actor
Influencer
Fashion designer
Circus ringmaster
Cruise ship entertainer
Opera singer
Comedian
Traffic warden
Cardiologist
Jewellery designer

Well-being

Ruled by the life-giving Sun, you're a high-energy person with an unquenchable zest for life. You take your exercise routine seriously, partly because you're a Fire sign, and will feel more relaxed when you've burned off some of that excess zeal – but typically it's looking good that is your biggest motivator.

Vigorous workouts and cardio routines keep your circulatory system ticking over, but you would rather be outside in the Sun and fresh air than cooped up in a gym or sports club. You can't keep a Lion indoors for long – unless they're sleeping. Having the undivided attention of a personal trainer might be something that's hard to resist as you'll be happy to impress someone who is there exclusively to encourage and praise you.

Big game player

Fun and games are a favourite Leo pastime, whether playing cards or Monopoly at home, or enjoying a sporting challenge where you can improve on your personal best, with activities like golf, tennis or interval training.

You're happiest when surrounded by other people, so being a member of a team will satisfy your social instincts. Football, basketball, hockey and most team sports will appeal, and, of course, you will aim to be the star player. You expect applause and praise but it's really your enthusiastic spirited approach and great organisational skills that make you such a valued player.

Taste for the finer things

If you could afford it, you'd probably choose to eat out most of the time. You get to show off your new outfit, talk to everyone and get seen in a fashionable spot. Besides, cooking and cleaning isn't really your thing. You do enjoy baking awesome-looking cakes because of the wow factor, but you'll leave all the washing up to someone else.

You prefer eating in company and your generosity and flamboyant taste make you a perfect dinner date. When you choose something from the menu, you're usually looking for the caviar, lobsters and oysters rather than anything modest or that you probably have in your own fridge back home. You'll plump for the fanciest dish on the menu and insist on buying everyone at the table drinks.

Party hard

Relaxing is a big deal for you, but even your down time can look pretty hectic to less energetic types. As the zodiac's favourite party animal, when you're out having fun you'll be on your feet until the music stops or everyone else leaves. But Lions need their sleep and you can get tetchy if you haven't had a proper lie-in for a few days.

VIRGO (24 August - 23 September)

Personality

You were born to create order in a chaotic world, to be of service to humanity by keeping everything in good working order: sharp, clean, polished and beautifully organised. You have a defined, natural ability to know how to put things right. If you are talking to someone who has a piece of fluff on their jacket, you may not be able to concentrate on what they're saying until you have removed it. You can't help but notice inconsistencies, mistakes and small flaws in your everyday life. Not out of any malice or antagonism towards others, but to improve life's functioning and make things run more smoothly for everyone.

Without you Virgo, the world would descend into madness. You're one of the most hardworking, conscientious signs of the zodiac – and certainly the most industrious. If anyone needs something done, or to understand how something works, they ask you first because they know they'll receive a sensible, practical, answer that's beautifully simple.

Virgo is the zodiac sign most associated with health and healing and you are likely very aware of your own body and the need to keep it in good condition. Sometimes your mercurial concern with health can spill over into hypochondria, but, more often than not, it translates as a keen interest in health and nutrition and a wish to keep yourself as pure and natural as possible.

Your astrological emblem, The Virgin, relates to your shyness, idealism and desire for perfection. The Virgin is usually depicted holding sheaves of wheat in her hands, symbolising the harvest in late summer – Virgo time. The wheat represents wisdom gathered from different fields of experience.

Quietly brilliant

For all you are the zodiac's know-it-all, you don't want to be the person making all the rules and are not a huge fan of being in the spotlight. Often observing the important details others leave behind (and often the unimportant ones, too!) you know how things ought to be done. But you lack a bit of confidence and boldness when it comes to getting others on board with your ideas.

Once you get over your modesty and are comfortable with the people around you, the communicative, Mercury-ruled side of your character makes an appearance and you can be very talkative. It's your lack of arrogance and willingness to adjust that make people warm to you and listen to your advice. Even if you don't realise it yourself – you're secretly the one in charge of everyone else in the zodiac.

Doing a proper job

You work extremely hard to help other people, or to contribute to a useful cause. You're happy to work on your own without praise or recognition, as long as you're working alongside others who you know appreciate what you're doing.

You don't *want* to do all the work, but it would irritate you far too much to leave it to someone else who wouldn't do as good a job. But, unfortunately for you, more unscrupulous types, also know you'll take care of things eventually and may even, occasionally, do things purposefully sloppily, knowing you will want to take that task off them next time.

Encouraging and exacting

A kind and helpful person, you're a perfectionist at heart and see it as your duty to help the people you love be the best they can. When you notice talent or aptitude in others, you instinctively want to encourage them to better themselves because you find wasted potential deeply upsetting. This desire for perfection and efficiency can sometimes mean you spend most of your time concentrating on things that aren't quite right or could be better.

You fuss and worry over little things and can't relax until you have reorganised and ordered what is in front of you. You're pernickety about your workspace, unable to settle into writing an email if your desk is untidy, or there's a coffee mug stain on your coaster. When you cook, you wash up and clean as you go, organising cupboards while food is in the oven. You can't lounge on the sofa until the dog's been fed, the washing machine is empty, the clothes are dry and everything's folded and put away. You probably have a very clean, tidy home but you rarely take time to appreciate it. And if you did, you'd probably notice that the walls need repainting or decide that old picture could do with a better frame.

self-compassion

You're a champion at singing other people's praises and helping them to grow and express their talents, but you keep your own mighty capabilities to yourself. Modest to your core, you can be extremely hard on yourself. The idea that you might be held up to others' criticism makes you feel very uneasy.

Above all, you are compelled to be honest and showing off in any way would be tantamount to declaring yourself perfect – something your own high standards just won't allow you to do. Even if your brilliance is obvious to everyone around you, you'll still have cause to doubt it.

Love and relationships

You are a naturally private person, so when you first realise you are attracted to another, it can take you a little by surprise. You are *picky*, but that's just because you know what you're looking for – so when you see someone who fits the bill, it's a bit unsettling. You might not even understand what you're supposed to do next.

You're naturally shy in love, and you often have a crush for a long time before you pluck up courage to act on it, if at all!

Prone to self-criticism, you'll probably have come up with a hundred reasons why your beloved won't be interested. You hold yourself to the same high standards you expect from a lover, and it can be difficult for you to live up to your own self-imposed rules. But if you could stand back and take an honest look at yourself or have a bit of faith in what others are telling you, then you may notice the charming, self-effacing, kind and talented person who everyone sees.

Thoughtful and attentive

Once in a relationship you are committed. Your planetary ruler, Mercury looks for friendship, and an intellectual rapport is crucial to the longevity of your partnership. You're a thoughtful, attentive lover and surprisingly, considering your virginal symbolism, when you're under the sheets, you're a passionate and adventurous lover.

You want your life together to be private and expect the same level of discretion from your partner. You won't be happy if you find out your other half has been posting pictures of your life together on social media and will even feel uncomfortable discussing details of your love life with your own friends and family.

You value honesty over flattery and will much rather hear constructive criticism instead of meaningless compliments. Knowing what your other half really thinks is far more important to you than being told what you want to hear, and it will bring you closer together.

For a truly blissful relationship, your partner ought to understand how your mind works. If he or she knows you well, they'll appreciate that for you to feel relaxed and focused on them, your environment should be neat and orderly. Your lover becomes much sexier in your eyes if they voluntarily take out the bins or dry the cutlery before putting it away. A self-respecting true Virgo will feel a thrill of satisfaction seeing their other half scrubbing grouting with bleach and a toothbrush.

Taking care of details

You notice all the little details about your partner, from where they buy their shoes to how they like their eggs, and which toothpaste they prefer. You show a touching concern that their lives are running smoothly, and readily offer them assistance. You take your routines and rituals seriously and expect your loved ones to feel the same way. If the person you adore always has crumpets for breakfast and you've only got porridge, you'll make an early morning trip to find crumpets. You'll have catalogued all your lover's favourite things and even when they're not sure which brand of socks they prefer, or which bag they like to take on holiday – you will have the answer.

Mercury-ruled people love to learn new things and to better themselves, so discovering a different language together, hiking or taking an interest in nutrition are all productive pastimes that will make you feel like you are both healthy and growing as a couple.

Perfect imperfections

You pursue perfection gently, perhaps even a little unconsciously. But it's important that you recognise this trait and make peace with it, because if you don't, it could drive you quite mad. Noticing small things that unsettle you can build imperceptibly until one day your partner accidentally sneezes over your dinner or leaves the nail clippers in the bed and bang – you're divorced! Deep down one of your biggest fears is that you are imperfect, and maybe that's why you're so harsh on yourself and exacting of the people around you. One of your greatest lessons is to accept your own failings, for when you do, you'll relax and be much more tolerant about everyone else's. Everyone is flawed and still lovable – even you!

Most compatible love signs

Pisces - Pisces hypnotises you with their unending faith in love and will help you let go and trust in life's essential goodness.

Virgo - as long as you are not too intellectually competitive, this ought to be a very stimulating and nurturing relationship.

Taurus - you have a similar work ethic and values, and agree that love as a life-long commitment.

Least compatible love signs

Aries - impulsive Fires signs prefer to do things rather than talk about them, so no long nights spent discussing your ingrown toenails with them, then.

Sagittarius - sweeping generalisations drive you potty and Sagittarius often has a number of them on hand.

Libra - you respect people with honest opinions that they stand by, and Libra changes theirs depending on who they last spoke to.

Work and Career

You're a hardworking problem solver, famed for your clear, uncluttered communication style. Meticulous by nature, you like to assimilate the task in front of you, piece by piece, and analyse the information in minute detail. Your thoroughness is unique in the workplace and when given a job to do, you treat it seriously. It might take a while longer to complete than the other zodiac signs, because you will correct and adjust every single error as you go, but the end results will be impeccable. This applies whether you're an accountant, florist or trombone player.

Being correct

If you're honest, Virgo, you probably realise you make more work for yourself than you need to. You are always busy, but you tend to be the only one adding things to your in-tray. It's your raison d'être to consider and evaluate, and your reverence for productivity can mean you labour over technicalities. Every stage of your work matters, and you have a logical thought-out opinion about what you're doing and why. But your conscientiousness can take up more time than you like, which just makes you more anxious that details might get missed if you rush it.

You're not an aggressive person by any means but if you think you are right (and you usually are) you won't back down. This is not because you are being antagonistic; it is because you are right!

Where you excel

Virgo is associated with health and healing, ensuring all the complex parts of the body are functioning properly together. Therefore, combining your Mercury-ruled capacity for knowledge with your earthy natural ability to work with something tangible in a career as a doctor, surgeon or nutritionist, would suit you well.

Your dedication and meticulous skills sees you excel in tasks which require detailed, or exacting standards. Science, maths, engineering and editing work would all satisfy your analytical brain and eagle-eyed abilities. Your discernment, discretion and grasp of minutiae would be an asset if you took up law, or even if you were appointed as a judge. After all, nobody loves the last word more than a Virgo!

Most compatible colleagues

Gemini- as you're both ruled by Mercury, you appreciate each other's superfast minds and have a shared love of pens, rulers and notebooks.

Cancer - you're both quietly industrious and enjoy the other's ability to work alone without needing much attention.

Capricorn - workaholic realists, together you will change the world for the better – without rest!

Least compatible colleagues

Sagittarius - pie in the sky thinking and wild generalisations make you want to cry.

Leo - too proud of their work – and it's usually yours!

Aquarius - you like to examine things carefully – Aquarius prefers balancing the stapler on their nose.

Ideal Virgo careers

Computer engineer
Laboratory assistant
Nutritionist
Lifecoach
Air traffic controller
Journalist
Accountant
Restaurant critic

LIBRA (24 September – 23 October)

Personality

You are an intellectual Air sign ruled by romantic, charming, Venus. As an Air sign you are one of the zodiac's thinkers and communicators, and with relationship-oriented Venus as your ruler, you crave harmonious rapport, balance and fairness with everyone you encounter. You are one of the most sociable signs of the zodiac, and your desire

to please others and dislike of conflict, means you sometimes s
acrifice your own ambitions to keep the peace. Your astrological
symbol is the Scales, representing your fair judgment, excellent taste
and love of symmetry. Because you are so concerned with making
the right decisions it can take you a long time to weigh up all the
options, but when you have made up your mind, it's usually set in
stone… unless too many people disagree with you, in which case
you may have to rethink!

Partnership quest

As the seventh of the 12 zodiac signs, you are the first to have an
opposite number, and your longing for a partner is one of your
strongest motivations. You were born to share, discuss and consider
your thoughts and feelings with others, and you need strong
relationships to make you feel more complete. It's natural for you to
ponder others' opinions before you make up your own mind – even
if you don't necessarily agree with them. Bouncing ideas back against
someone else somehow makes your own thoughts feel more solid
and real. You find it easier to see yourself through the eyes of other
people, and so their good opinion seems essential if you are to have
good opinion of yourself.

To help you discover who you really are, you may, quite
unconsciously, see others as a mirror. This can sometimes mean you
remain with a partner for far too long, hoping that either things will
improve, or just out of the fear of being alone. However, when you
let yourself explore different types or relationships with a variety of
people, you will discover how you differ from them, and what makes
you unique. It's often a balancing act between you and others, and
your thoughts and emotions. But weighing things up is what you
were born to do!

Venusian aesthete

Both Taurus and Libra are Venus-ruled and have a deep appreciation
for beauty and the finer things in life. Taurus is an Earth sign, so
their love tends to be expressed through a desire for tangible things,
such as food, comfort and money. In Air sign Libra, your Venusian

sensibilities are conveyed though the expression of ideas – intellectual compatibility, wit, excellent manners, refined tastes, intelligence and appearance. You can be quite particular about how you decorate and beautify your environment – and yourself!

You may refuse to answer the door if you think you're looking shabby. Even in a hospital bed you'll be the cute one with shiny hair, stylish pajamas, designer stubble or full make-up. You dress well and are a dedicated follower of fashion, enjoying colour, eye-catching designs and sumptuous fabrics. Style usually trumps comfort in your eyes, and you'll plump for gorgeous shoes over uglier, more practical varieties every time. Your luxury-loving Venusian tastes often stretch your budget but you'll gladly go into the red for a beautiful bit of tailoring. You have an outfit for every occasion and you always notice what other people are wearing.

Your environment needs to reflect your refined tastes, too, and your home will be a clutter-free, peaceful space, artfully decorated and aesthetically pleasing. Fresh flowers, candles and some contemporary works of art will adorn your perfectly painted walls.

Balanced opinion

As you are the sign of balance and the zodiac's diplomat, you insist you hear all sides of a story before deciding what the fairest course of action should be. An excellent listener, you empathise with everyone's account and don't take immediate action before you have considered all options.

People-pleasing is such second nature to you that you lose sight of your own power to decide where to go, and with whom. Your exceptional tolerance can sometimes lead others to take advantage of your good nature or they might assume you will always back them up. Often fearing to rock the boat too much, less scrupulous individuals can become frustrated with your passivity, and can goad you into making decisions that you're not quite ready for.

Always giving people the benefit of the doubt is an admirable personality trait, as long as you are dealing with people who have equally high morals. At some point in your life you may find yourself in a far from perfect relationship or situation, where you have continued uncomplaining and forgiving for months or years. On an unconscious level you may have been registering that things are not working, but the scales haven't quite tipped one way or the other. Then, quite out of the blue, after a small disagreement, you suddenly tip – your mind is made up and there's no going back.

Love and relationships

You're an old-fashioned romantic Libra, and you want the whole fairytale! You're an intellectual Air sign ruled by Venus, the love and relationship planet, so searching for romantic fulfilment is a crucial part of your existence. Libra is the sign of partnership, of looking at the world from outside of oneself, and a true Libra longs to meet their soulmate.

You love the drama and ceremony of romance, and you absolutely expect to find it. Though, because this is such an important decision, you may take an inordinately long time to make up your mind about exactly what you're looking for. It's just too important a decision to be made lightly.

Thoughtful and affectionate

Your attractive, sociable personality and comely smile ensure you won't be short of admirers. If someone takes your fancy, you'll weigh up the pros and cons before finding out more about him or her. You take great pleasure in the more genteel aspects of courtship, but you can be extremely seductive when you're attracted to someone – and very hard to resist!

Your intended will be able to keep you entertained with their wit, and as a loquacious Air sign you get a kick out of sending flirty messages back and forth. A potential partner has to appeal to you mentally, perhaps even as something of a fantasy figure, before you'll up your game.

The excitement of the initial swoony passion of a new love affair, where you both crash into lamp posts daydreaming of the other, is your rose-tinted Libra idea of heaven. Once you've weighed up all the possibilities and decided to go for it, you shower your other half with love and attention. You are thoughtful and affectionate and always thinking up way to please the one you adore.

Blissful harmony

Disliking chaos, discord and negativity, you are very sensitive to any of your partner's criticisms and you worry about what they really think. It's important for you both to be able to talk candidly at the start of a relationship and to pledge always to communicate. You need reassurance that everything is going well, and you can become resentful if you're on the end of any silent treatment without knowing precisely why. You must feel that you're an equal partner and are not solely responsible for your beloved's good – or bad – moods.

Togetherness is your favourite thing and snuggling up on the sofa with your other half for a lazy night in is one of your favourite things, as long as there's good quality nibbles, wine, and an arty film in the offing. But you also love showing your lover off. You're a sociable type who enjoys dressing up to be seen in the hottest places and you'll want to share the glam high life with your chosen companion.

Avoiding confrontation

You feel deeply unsettled by angry scenes, chaos and noise, so shy away from conflict or arguments. If your partner says something harsh, or if they're loud and angry you find it really difficult to respond. Arguments and ugly scenes have you running for the hills. Your politeness prevents you from being outspoken, even when you feel you ought to be sticking up for yourself. It feels so uncomfortable when your sense of harmony is disrupted that you'll make the peace as quickly as possible – even if you're not the person in the wrong.

Your fear of confrontation can occasionally be used against you by less scrupulous types, and not being able to voice your anger can make you feel powerless. Being completely honest with your lover is a challenge, not only because of the unbearable tension, but because of your indecisiveness and unwillingness to take any action.

Telling others exactly where you stand is probably a skill you'll learn from experience. But life will get easier once you realise that the sky doesn't fall down if you voice an opinion, and others will respect you for being honest.

Most compatible love signs

Gemini – the good-natured banter you share will keep you both in stitches and you'll always be able to surprise each other.

Aquarius – sociable Aquarius enjoys your wit and charm and learns from your people-pleasing skills, while Aquarius teaches you how to be less concerned about what others think.

Leo – you're a two-person party! You both love the limelight and being seen at your best, but you can laze about in style together, too.

Least compatible love signs

Cancer – you have some trouble understanding each other's emotions as your feelings propel you towards people while Cancer's make them scuttle away.

Capricorn – solemn Capricorns make you laugh with their dry sense of humour but they're naturally reserved and haughty where you're effusive and open.

Virgo – you get on well as friends, as you both appreciate excellent craftsmanship and notice details others miss, but Virgo's a realist and you're a romantic.

Work and career

Behind your sweet, sociable personality, lies a shrewd business brain. As one of the zodiac's most skilled communicators you understand how to persuade people to work togethe. Well-liked in the workplace you go out of your way to please your co-workers, and easily make friends at the office. Colleagues know you to be a friendly, chilled and witty character, and you're actually surprisingly cool and logical when faced with stressful or complicated tasks.

Creating a harmonious world

Your Venusian ruler compels you to create a more harmonious and beautiful world. Artistic and creative, you have an affinity with good design and your eye for colour and desire for pleasant surroundings might spur you on to become an interior designer or architect, and many Libra work in the music and fashion industries. The beauty industry may appeal too, especially if combined with more social aspects of the job. Life as a make-up artist, costume designer, hairdresser or masseuse, should be enjoyable as you could combine your social and artistic abilities.

Fair boss

You're a very friendly, sociable boss, not altogether comfortable being the one making all the difficult decisions. You can labour over the smallest choices, but when you make your judgement, your opinion is usually nuanced and well-respected. You make it very easy for your co-workers to communicate with you, and honest opinions are heartily encouraged.

Your clever charm means you can turn someone down for a pay rise but have them leave your office feeling better about themselves than when they went in. Less charitable colleagues may say your friendliness can get in the way of your work, but the opposite is usually true. When you need something done, people around you are happy to help, as they'll be keen to repay past favours.

Most compatible colleagues

Taurus - you're both Venus-ruled and understand that paying for a bon vivant lifestyle, requires diligence and determination.

Aries – you have an understanding that you're happy to do all the good-cop charming stuff, as long as they can take care of the shouty, bossy bits.

Libra - this is a great working relationship because you're on the same level, so when one of you is down, the other balances you back up again.

Least compatible colleagues

Scorpio – Scorpio can be something of a closed book at work, so you're never really sure where you stand or what their opinions are.

Aquarius – you have great fun together but when you need Aquarius to respect your authority they might behave like a sulky teenager.

Capricorn – Capricorns are suspicious of charming, people-pleasers and you're suspicious of skeptical lugubrious types.

Ideal Libra Careers

Human resources
Relationship counsellor
Web designer
Make-up artist
Fashion designer
Public relations consultant
Hairdresser
Art dealer
Wedding planner
Lawyer

Well-being

You love to look hot, Libra, and it can be a challenge for you to balance your love of food and a full social life, with a limiting diet or rigorous exercise plan. Venus-ruled signs are usually well-groomed and spend a great deal of care on their appearance, so getting hot, sweaty and breathless won't be your first choice when it comes to staying active. Ugliness disturbs you, and you can be harsh on yourself if you catch an unflattering glimpse of your puffy, straining face in a mirror.

Food and drink

Venus is a planet of enjoyment, and food will be high on your agenda. Venus-ruled Taurus and Libra both have quite slow metabolisms and are prone to gaining weight. Sweets, puddings and carbs are one of your greatest pleasures, but obviously there is a downside to all those delicious treats - it's hard to be disciplined when there's such an abundance of delicious goodies on show.

Balance is the key to your well-being, and your passion for indulgent food may be difficult to master, but there is a middle road. Air signs dislike feeling heavy after rich food, as it saps your vitality and makes you feel lazy. You can address the sluggishness by eating smaller, portions and keeping your food choices interesting. Or perhaps when you are at home, you can decide to prepare healthier but tasty options for yourself but choose whatever you fancy from the menu when you're out for dinner.

Friendly activities

The gym doesn't hold much appeal – unless it's a cool place to hang out, in which case you'll enjoy spending time in the cafe, chatting to friends and blowing your hard-earned calories over lunch. If you do venture onto some machines, you'll be wearing the latest kit and will sneak a good look at what other people are wearing, too. Tennis and squash, or any sports or activity requiring a partner, will suit your need to work with someone else, so ballroom dancing, Zumba, and water-aerobic classes appeal too.

To relax and unwind, chatting with friends is your preferred way to chill. Talking out any problems and knowing that someone else understands where you're coming from is the best therapy. Counselling can also work brilliantly for you if you wish to express what's on your mind directly, without worrying about offending anyone or being too polite about how you really feel.

SCORPIO
(24 October – 22 November)

Personality

Your reputation precedes you, Scorpio. Hypnotic, sexy and mysterious with that violent sting in your tail – you appear to have all of the zodiac's most extreme and exciting personality traits. But where do these dark and dubious characteristics come from?

Scorpio is a Water sign, which is associated with strong emotions. Your planetary ruler is deep, dark, powerful Pluto, the lord of the underworld, controlling all that lies below the surface. The positive side of Pluto is that he pulls things from the dark into the light, so they can be transformed and healed. The darker side of Pluto reveals an obsession with power and control, which brings up deep passions: possessiveness, jealousy and revenge. Like your zodiac symbol, the Scorpion, you prefer to hide yourself and keep your motives secret, but you will strike if you are threatened.

Dark horse

Enmeshed in dark myths and dramatic life-or-death symbolism, it's forgivable to imagine Scorpio to be heartless and cruel. But your tough exterior is just armour that protects your deeply sensitive Water sign heart. You feel your emotions very deeply, but you won't let just anyone see you vulnerable. You have a knack for unearthing other people's emotional weak spots and remembering just where to hurt them if they betray you in future. So, no, you won't display your softer side, at least not without a reciprocal exchange of vulnerabilities. It's a little like owning a nuclear deterrent. When you really trust someone, they'll know where you hurt, and you'll know where they hurt. If one of you pushes the other's button, you'll destroy each other. But it takes you a long time to get to that stage of trust.

Trust me, I'm a Scorpio

You're a secretive person and it serves you well. When you gain someone's trust you take it as an honour. If a friend wishes to share that they're actually a spy or enjoy dressing up as a chicken for kicks, you'll take this knowledge to the grave. You keep secrets because knowledge is power, and, who knows – you may need to use it against them one day. But much more likely, you keep schtum because trust is everything to you. That's why you rely on so few people yourself. You'll enjoy hearing salacious gossip as much as anyone, but you treat real secrets with the utmost respect… and you will have a few of your own.

The power of money

Scorpio is one of the financial zodiac signs, the other being your opposite number, Taurus. As a Pluto person you respect the power of money and your relationship to it can be complicated. You're smart and shrewd, and you tend to make money easily, and Scorpio is also associated with inheritance, so you may benefit from a legacy of some sort. You're quite secretive about how much money you make and won't be the one in the office discussing your annual bonus or how much your salary went up or down. But you'll be very interested in what other people are earning.

Emotional depth

You're not frightened of your emotions, but because you feel them so keenly, you are often at their mercy. You're not an escapist, and you know for sure the only way to tackle uncomfortable emotions is to do the hardest thing of all, you must face the source of the pain, bring it to its knees, look in its eyes and then ask it honestly what it needs. There's no point in lying because you're just hiding from yourself. You can take it, and many Scorpios find themselves in counselling, locating the source of their troubles, so they can master their pain and avoid similar situations in future. You hate that others can have so much control over you but eventually you transform whatever brought you pain into a source of power. And that's why you always win!

Losing yourself

When you get interested in a subject, idea or a person, you become quite obsessive. You're the person that binge watches episodes of a dark, gripping TV series, who stays up all night reading an absorbing detective story or the one who has a sudden fascination with hypnosis or mysticism. Your fascination with sex isn't purely physical. You long to merge with someone else, to be possessed and lose your sense of individuality in a uniting of souls, to be reborn again. You don't just want sex, you're on a quest to attain a higher level of consciousness. No pressure on your partner then!

Love and relationships

In love you're all or nothing. Pluto-ruled people aren't wishy-washy or coy, but you have undeniable sex appeal. You're sultry and moody and when you're attracted to someone new, you hint at the passionate depths you're usually so keen to conceal. Your clothes tend to be plain in darker colours, but you choose sensual fabrics with a touch of drama, a subtle shine, velvet trim or an upturned collar. But it's your alluring, magnetic eyes that really draw people in. Sometimes your intensity can make people feel a little uncomfortable, but it's not intentional. You look directly into people's eyes for a fraction too long, often quite unconsciously, because that's where you discover their most precious secrets. Some people feel exposed in your gaze, while others enjoy feeling seen.

Subtle signals

Seductive but subtle, when you're attracted to someone your feelings will be strong, but you probably won't want to show your hand for a while. You like to watch from afar, noticing all the intimate details of the person who has captured your attention. You take in the way they move, how they use their hands when they speak and the timbre of his or her voice. You may be having a conversation, but you've lost the thread because you've been staring at their knees, neck or lips and wondering what it would be like to kiss them. You may try to keep your feelings to yourself, but your eyes will give you away. You have a hypnotic intensity when you're looking at someone you want, and that longing stare may reveal your real feelings.

You'll be looking for signs of reciprocation, but because you're so subtle, the other person may have picked up a vibe but won't be entirely sure.

Serious passions

You take love seriously and don't make it easy for others to get close to you. The trust and security must be real before you let down your defences. As the zodiac's most passionate sign, you give yourself to your partner completely. For you sex isn't purely physical, it's an all-consuming, profound spiritual union and a release of powerful reserves of emotional energy. This is not something you take lightly as your lover will see you at your most vulnerable, so you will need plenty of reassurance that this will last forever.

Contrary to your reputation as a philanderer, you have a deep need for security and permanence in your relationships. Sex *is* essential to you, but you're no flash in the pan. If the love is real, you commit every fibre of your being to your partner loyally and, at times, almost obsessively. You can become possessive of your partner if they give cause to make you feel insecure, and can become very jealous, if provoked. But emotionally, you give everything, so if your partner cheats, shames you or breaks your heart, you will want revenge. And the best revenge of all is to find a way not to care.

Going into the well

You work harder than any other zodiac sign to repair yourself if you've been emotionally wounded. Because you are so brave and honest with yourself, you have the power to regenerate, heal and to put yourself back stronger than before. But, in order to be reborn, first you have to die. You do this by fully experiencing your pain, re-living it, feeling the emotions as fully as possible, giving yourself over to the truth of the loss, rejection, fear or anger. You go deep into the well of feeling, then you analyse yourself over and over for a way through. You don't always find easy answers, and sometimes there are none, but eventually, sometimes after many years, you come out healed and transformed.

Most compatible love signs

Cancer - sensitive, intuitive Cancer can provide you with the security and reassurance you seek and can read your changing moods.

Taurus – the Taurus languid, slow, sensuous approach to life masks inner passions that attract and intrigue you.

Capricorn - responsible, steady goat people won't spring any surprises on you emotionally, and they're usually quite sensible with money.

Least compatible love signs

Libra - you're too hot to handle for superficial Libra who likes things to be nice rather than terrifyingly passionate and sweaty.

Leo - the king of brash meets the king of subtle – you're made of different stuff and won't see eye to eye for long.

Aries - you like self-belief and boldness of Aries, but they lack your emotional finesse, which you can find quite annoying.

Work and career

Strong-willed and magnetic, you're a motivated self-starter with an aura of mystery. Perfectly self-controlled, you never give away what you're thinking. You're a bit of a loner in your job, disliking being in the spotlight, and your co-workers may even be a little suspicious of you. But that's just because you give them so little to go on.

Workmates who get to know you better, sense your empathy and discretion, and may find themselves spilling their hearts to you. Trustworthy to your core, any gossip that finds its way to your desk will be kept strictly to yourself.

Scorpio for hire

Discreet, professional and intuitive, any work where you have to research, analyse or dig deep to discover more information will suit your detective brain. Employment which involves consumer psychology, counselling or any element of negotiation, suits your love of getting to the heart of what really motivates people.

Scorpio has a talent for merging with others in money-making ventures and you would find banking, accounting, estate agency, or any position where you make a commission from other people's investments, very satisfying.

Closed book

There's no problem you can't solve, and your professional manner demands respect without ever asking for it. You rarely raise your voice to anyone in your charge, but there's an edge to you that suggests you might. You give away little about your own life, yet you miss nothing about what your employees get up to. They'll have to be far more devious if they believe they can pull the wool over your eyes, and you'll spot when they're on social media or pretending to work when they're actually shopping.

You don't make a big deal of minor transgressions, but you'll create a mental note of them in case they come in useful at a later date.

Most compatible colleagues
Sagittarius - unlike you, Sagittarius is open and honest, and you know exactly who you're dealing with – and how to manipulate them!

Aries - these guys can be childish and aggressive, but you definitely want them on your side in a fight or competition.

Virgo - you respect the modest, conscientious Virgo manner. You know if the pair of you work together that you're a quietly devastating team.

Least compatible colleagues
Scorpio - you tolerate each other if you're working toward the same goal, but if you're enemies, forget it; you'll both perish trying to outmanoeuvre each other.

Aquarius - great fun to be around and have genius ideas, but they're unlikely to respect your authority.

Leo - talk too much, need too much praise, and can't work unsupervised.

Ideal Scorpio Careers
Negotiator
Spy
Detective
Tax consultant
Police force
Funeral director
Researcher
Psychologist
Miner
Investment banker

Well-being
Ruled by Pluto, the powerhouse planet of extremes, your metabolism is usually high. Your calm exterior masks your intensely emotional

nature, which must have a healthy outlet, otherwise you can get tense and lose your cool – and nobody's comfortable with an annoyed Scorpio around!

One of the most important things you can do for your health is to talk to someone about your feelings. You have such a rich and intense emotional life, but you keep things very much to yourself. If you don't feel you can express yourself to a friend or partner, going for counselling or psychotherapy will be a therapeutic experience where you can safely bare your soul.

You rarely do half measures and can be quite obsessive about your health – as in taking things to excessive lengths. You're driven, energetic and competitive but you usually prefer to work out on your own. Extreme sports and adrenaline boosters such as rock climbing, skiing, cave diving and kite surfing will help you channel repressed or challenging feelings and relieve stress and help move any blocked energy.

Food and drink

Your take-it-or-leave-it attitude sees you swing from being obsessed with one type of food to being off your kibbles completely. You tend to enjoy foods that others turn their nose up at – intense dark chocolate, bitter cocktails, and pungent blue cheeses. Spicy, hot, energy-giving foods such as curries, chilli and hot pepper sauce give you a satisfying kick, and you'll experiment with anything exotic, pungent or dark and delightful.

Scorpio's dark, moody, dangerous energy makes you the zodiac's 'sex, drugs, and rock'n'roll' character. This isn't so much for the escapism – you're far too self-aware for that – it's more in the spirit of curiosity and experimentation. A character of extremes, you can push things a little too far. You want to know what life is like on the wild side and you may sometimes end up in some darker places than you originally intended. But then you counter this by living like a monk for weeks after any serious blow-outs.

You may be a little obsessive about your weight and have probably already learned from experience that extreme or yo-yo dieting doesn't do you any good. You get a hundred percent involved with what you're doing, so you have less trouble sticking to cabbage soup diets, ridiculously low-calorie plans or pineapple-only type fads. You can be too disciplined for a while, then ping the other way and live like King Henry VIII for a few weeks to make up for it.

SAGITTARIUS
(23 November – 21 December)

Personality

You are a frank, enthusiastic and carefree Fire sign, and your astrological symbol is the Archer or Centaur – a mythological creature, half man, half horse. You have an impulsive and paradoxical personality, and your character represents the balancing act between the animal side of human nature and the human search for meaning.

Legend has it that you would shoot your arrow, gallop to where it landed, then shoot again – eventually covering the entire globe – delighting in every new experience to which your arrow led you.

You adore travelling and are always ready to explore new territory and meet people from different backgrounds and cultures. You live for fun and adventure and tackle any of life's challenges with a smile on your face, and a hearty belly laugh. With fortunate, gregarious Jupiter as your ruling planet, you're a popular, cheerful soul who plunges fearlessly, and sometimes a little recklessly, into the deep end of whatever life throws at you.

Freedom to explore

Above all, you desire the freedom to explore and experience life as fully as possible, and you're at your happiest at the beginning of a new journey, project or romance. Your initial enthusiasm and absolute belief in what you are doing propels you forwards with tremendous force. You have a rough and ready energy, more bluff and blunder than a thoughtful, refined approach – some may even call you clumsy! But the sheer optimism and friendly openness you apply to everything you tackle can be very refreshing.

Independent thinker

Your ruling planet, jovial Jupiter, is associated with luck, optimism and abundance, and assures you have plenty of confidence in your own abilities. Many Sagittarians excel at sport, as you love the challenge of being told something is not possible, and then proving everyone wrong. Sheer belief often takes you further than agility or technique and few have your passion, courage and optimism when it comes to trouncing the competition. You have a powerful physique – not quite graceful, but sturdy, strong and energetic.

Philosophical and religious matters will fascinate you throughout your life. You may have experienced others' strict religious beliefs as a child, and grown up questioning these ideas, or found religion yourself and use it as a guiding light. One thing's for sure, you don't like being told what to believe in or how to live by anyone whether they're parents, teachers, friends or the Government.

Blunt or just honest?

Your craving for authenticity means you can be a little 'on the nose' when giving your opinion – which you do frequently. For you the truth is a dish served without a coating of sugar and you expect the people in your life to be as blunt with you, as you are with them.

Luckily your uncomplicated approach is appreciated by more people than it offends, as your loved ones will know exactly where they stand – and know they can be just as honest about your faults as you are of theirs... in theory. However, another one of your contradictions is that you're not as open to criticism as you are at dishing it out. As the zodiac's truth hunter, you feel you've earned the authority to be right, and you enjoy a good verbal battle with anyone who disagrees with you. It winds you up when people challenge your intelligence because your wisdom is real, and hard-won. You've studied and understood and explored, and righteously feel you have put in the work to be right.

Humour and passion

You have a colourful, effusive, humorous way of communicating with people, gesticulating and bringing your stories to life, while persuading even die-hard sceptics over to your way of thinking. You are a warm, charismatic and engaging speaker and have little trouble in attracting romantic interest. An idealist to your core, you absolutely believe in the power of love and are ever optimistic that you'll find it.

You can have quite a passionate, fiery relationship with the people closest to you because you can be quite dogmatic in your own beliefs

Extravagant spender

Money can be something of a sore point for Sagittarius has lusty spending habits. Hating to be restricted or restrained, especially when it comes to fun, you cheerfully spend money as quickly as you make it. You tend towards making bold or even risky decisions with your finances and will probably have burned your fingers more than once, when you've either gambled or invested unwisely. But again, you're a paradoxical creature and your ruler Jupiter is the luckiest planet of all!

Just when you're down to your last pennies, your fortunes can change, and you're back in the black again. But as budgeting or spending wisely often entails not eating the most expensive meals, or shopping less, or cutting down on holidays, you may have to cut back on some extravagant habits - not easy for a person with no boundaries!

Love and relationships

Half horse and half human, you're a creature of contradictions, striving for a balance between your animal instincts and enlightened thinking and love can tear you in two directions. Intellectual compatibility is essential, though you're a serious epicurean, and lust after more earthly pleasures, too.

You value your freedom very deeply, so thinking that you may be in love with someone can bring up mixed feelings and will awaken your questioning, philosophical nature. You may initially think it's a passing fad. You'll question yourself and you might ponder what being in love actually means, whether romantic love is so different to any other kind of love and, if it isn't so different, why does romantic love scare the pants off you? Do you think you can be in love and still see other people, or take off on your own for long periods of time? Do lovers still get married these days? Do I want children? Do I want children with this person? There's a great deal to contemplate, but when it comes right down to it – you're as easily bitten by the love bug as anyone else!

Natural exuberance

Whether initially you're drawn to a person's beautiful mind, or it's pure animal attraction, for you to be truly interested in someone romantically they have to be pretty special, because you are so deeply curious about everyone in your life.

You throw yourself into everything you do with the subtlety of a bulldozer, so your intended will have to be in real denial not to notice your romantic overtures. You're flirtatious and warm and you love to play the clown. Big on jokes, puns and generally playing the fool, you can be boisterous, loud and clumsy, and very hard to ignore. But it's your optimism and enormous appetite for life that wins the heart of whoever you have your arrow trained on. If you receive the slightest encouragement from the object of your affection, you'll gallop at speed towards them.

Pleasure principle

It may be true that only fools rush in, and as you're an idealistic daydreamer in love, your eyes may not be fully open when you first offer someone your heart. But your blind faith and good humour help you navigate most relationship ups and downs. Your optimism is infectious, and you'll soon win over even the coldest hearts. An easy-going, generous type, you want to share your whole world with your lover and for them to experience life's adventures and challenges together. A true Epicurean, you seek pleasure in all forms and boast an enormous appetite for food, sex, laughter and fun, and you'll generously shower your partner with all of life's delights.

When everything you do is larger than life, and your hopes are so cloud-high, it's only a matter of time before your rose-tinted spectacles fall from your nose and the object of so much adoration falls from their pedestal. Your Fire sign passion is sometimes short-lived and your wanderlust can return once things have cooled to a friendly sizzle. A cosy, comfortable kind of love isn't terribly exciting for you as a creature of such restless extremes, and you can be painfully blunt when your feelings have changed.

Painfully honest

Extremely generous in love, you expect only one thing in return – 100% honesty. You keep your end of the bargain by being scrupulously, painfully honest with your partner. Your truths tend to be delivered bluntly with scant regard for your loved one's feelings. Unless your partner is also a no-frills loving Sagittarius, you're going to bruise a few egos and may even break a few hearts along the way. And if you're really honest, which you are to your core, you'll have to admit that sometimes you're just spoiling for a fight or looking for an excuse to move on to pastures new.

Most compatible love signs

Leo - you're both generous, warm and have big hearts, Leos are one of the few zodiac signs who lives up to your high expectations.
Libra - you're intellectually well-matched, sociable and fair-minded and don't shy away from having a heated discussion.
Gemini - witty, funny and clever, the pair of you never tire of talking to each other, whether you're gossiping about friends or searching for the meaning of life.

Least compatible love signs

Scorpio - Scorpio's secretive nature frustrates and scares you a little – what's so bad or good that it can't be explored openly and honestly?
Cancer - where you are reckless and brave, Cancer is defensive and suspicious – you can definitely teach each other something, but romantically it's a damp squib.
Virgo - you enjoy Virgo's sharp intellect, but they're too anxious about trivial details for you to feel relaxed around them.

Work and career

Everyone needs an optimistic, cheerful, enterprising Sagittarian in the workplace. You light up the office with your infectious enthusiasm and willingness to take on any challenge. Your belief in yourself, and the projects you're involved, with carries everyone forward, even if you sometimes lose interest over the less exciting aspects such as budgeting or planning detailed schedules.

Principled to the end, you'll stick up for yourself if you feel unfairly treated, and if you're feeling unhappy at work you might even rock the boat a little to change the direction things are going in.

Physical or intellectual?
A contradictory character, there are usually two kinds of Sagittarius – academics or physically sporty types. Careers that satisfy your thirst for knowledge include teaching, whether sharing skills with youngers in school, or as a lecturer, professor or expert in a particular area. You're deeply intrigued by what drives people to accept particular ideas and reject others. Spiritual or humanitarian vocations such as being employed as a charity aid worker, minister, counsellor or politician would satisfy your hankering for meaningful knowledge and study.

Sports-obsessed Sagittarius are enthusiastic, encouraging coaches and trainers.

Sagittarius at the top
Sagittarius are happier being the boss than they are at towing the line. Outgoing, reasonable and capable of immense vision, you are natural leadership material. You're the perfect person to be in charge of an overarching message as you never lose sight of what it is you're trying to achieve on a grander scale.

Although impatient when you're bored, you never get tired of hearing your own voice, especially if you are explaining how other people ought to be doing something.

Most compatible colleagues
Aquarius - they give you the freedom and space you need to be creative because the know you'll come up with the goods.
Scorpio - unlikely friends outside the office, they're brilliant at handling money and resources, most of which you cheerfully gamble away!

Virgo - ruthlessly efficient Virgo spots all the important details you're missing in the bigger picture; without these guys on board, you're toast!

Least compatible colleagues

Capricorn - your optimistic and egalitarian approach to work doesn't sit well with these cautious, gloomy characters.

Taurus - you become impatient with slow Taurus, who needs too much time to adjust to change, they'll just dig in their heels and refuse to move.

Cancer - sensitive, caring Crabs are too easily bruised by your candid take on life.

Ideal Sagittarius Careers

Travel agent
Salesperson
Sports coach
Entrepreneur
Teacher
Theologian
Overseas aid worker
Spiritual guru
Politician
Explorer

Well-being

If you're a sporty, speedy, gym-loving Sagittarius, you'll be robust, energetic and competitive. Athletics and team games provide a natural outlet to burn off some of that excess Fire sign spirit. Hiking, rock climbing and sailing all appeal to your hale and hearty love for outdoor travel should prove exciting enough to hold your attention. You're naturally speedy, love a challenge and have the complete faith in your abilities. An excellent teacher, you are an inspiring coach and role model and enjoy encouraging others to achieve their personal bests.

If you're more of a thoughtful type of Sagittarian, who prefers your travel to be more mental than physical, you'll be an avid reader, with an insatiable curiosity about the people around you. But you're probably less interested in physical exercise. Luckily almost all Sagittarians find walking to be therapeutic as it stimulates the mind and the body, soothes your restlessness, and satisfies your curiosity to see what's around the next corner.

Food and drink

Your enormous appetite for life extends to food and drink, which you enjoy in large quantities. Your ruling planet Jupiter is associated with expansion and taking things too far, so you'll find it tricky not to overindulge in the good things. Your ruler, Jupiter, isn't terribly discriminating in its tastes, he just wants to expand what is on offer. You're a quantity rather than quality person, a supermarket shopper rather than a specialist grocer – or even better – both! Imagine a medieval banquet with an enormous table creaking with ample portions of meat, jellies, rich puddings, fruit, wine and beer – that's your kind of dinner.

As a party-loving creature of excess, you loathe limiting yourself when you're having a good time, and of course that will probably include enjoying a few beers, glasses of wine and strong cocktails. You can drink most other zodiac signs under the table, but you'll probably have already learned the hard way that some excesses are more of a headache than others.

More is more!

Of course, all this overindulgence and love of rich foods leads to steady weight gain, and if you're not the sporty Sagittarian type you'll have a propensity to become a little girthy. Sagittarians aren't usually lithe and lean and, unless you're very athletic, you'll have a jovial Jupiter rotundness to your body. Watching your weight does not come naturally as you rebel against any form of restraint and can be quite undisciplined when it comes to sticking to rules around food.

CAPRICORN
(22 December – 20 January)

Personality

You are a realistic, practical and hardworking person – the most ambitious character in the zodiac. The astrological symbol for Capricorn is the Goat, sometimes depicted as a mythical sea goat. The Goat represents your patient determination to scale great heights and reach the pinnacle in all your endeavours. You have lofty goals and the intelligence and diligence to achieve them. As an Earth sign you are pragmatic and stoical, firmly rooted in the tangible world, and you trust in what you can see, touch and build. Responsible, structure-loving Saturn is your ruling planet, which gives you a realistic, if slightly cynical, outlook on life. You expect to work very hard to achieve success and respect others who have set a good example.

Self-reliant and responsible

Capricorns tend to start life with an old head on young shoulders and lighten up as they age. Stern Saturn often presents Capricorns with challenges early in life and you may have had to shoulder extra responsibilities or encountered limiting circumstances. The humbler your beginnings, the greater your determination to overcome any challenges on the rocky road up the mountain. And in dealing with character-forming situations so young, you learned to become self-reliant. You are confident in your ability to succeed, but Saturn probably left you with a few niggly self-esteem issues, or a feeling of insecurity, which you'll be determined to mask by flinging yourself into a constant state of refinement and improvement.

Clever with money

As a sensible, accumulative Earth sign, you're excellent with money. You're not a frivolous spender. With a mature head on your shoulders, you're not about to waste the money you put so much time and energy into creating. One of the main reasons you're such a financial whizz is that you know when to act. You don't procrastinate, and you don't make excuses – you have a plan and you stick to it. It might not be rocket science, but surprisingly few people have the common sense or discipline to plough through tasks in quite the same way.

With an eye for the things that stand the test of time, Capricorns make excellent art and antique dealers, estate agents and jewellers. Yours isn't a boom or bust zodiac sign and you'll make your fortune slowly, over a long period of time. Even financially embarrassed Capricorns will have a business plan or two carefully tucked away, waiting for the right moment.

Traditional and sophisticated

Although cautious with money, when you feel secure enough, you'll wish to show the world that you've made it. You have excellent taste and want to look and sound like you mean business. A traditionalist at heart, you have something of a formal manner and conservative appearance. Dressed to impress in darker colours, timeless designer suits and tasteful accessories, you're usually impeccably presented, with neat hair and an imposing air of sophistication.

You like old money style in fashion, furnishings and the arts, leaning towards classical music and opera rather than jazz or pop, and you'll swoon at the ballet, rather than stage dive into a rock concert mosh pit.

Forever climbing

Authoritative Saturn ensures you feel comfortable at the helm in any business. Your drive, knowledge and sheer hard work eventually propel you to the top of your game and, as you've been headed up that mountain most of your life, it's naturally where you feel most confident and secure. Whether you find yourself as a CEO, the head of a small company or as a self-made entrepreneur, you are happy being the person accountable for making all the important, or final, decisions.

Not everyone wishes to be tethered to their job, or cares as much about their public persona, and it can get lonely up there. You'll have made many acquaintances and enjoy a plethora of colleagues and co-workers, so romance may have taken something of a back seat while you concentrated on your career.

Better with age

Nobody could accuse you of coming across as too gushy! Capricorns usually have tight reign over their emotions or are uncomfortable expressing their more complicated feelings. For all your polished exterior, you're not quite as at ease with your inner world but, again, you tend to form an easier relationship with your emotions as you get older.

As you are such a perfectionist, you should guard against becoming so caught up in chasing a particular dream or ambition to the exclusion of everything else, because if things don't work out as planned, Saturn can make you be very hard on yourself. It's vitally important you don't get sucked into a negative spiral, as you'll probably dwell far too long on what you could have done to improve things – even if it no longer matters.

Love and relationships

Nobody can accuse you of wearing rose-tinted spectacles when it comes to love and romance. As one of the most practical Earth signs in the zodiac, you're not about to leap up and down proclaiming your affections from the rooftops. At least not until you've thoroughly checked their reputation and background on social media, found out if they have a car, and what their future plans involve. You do have a slightly unfair reputation for being too status-conscious when it comes to choosing a partner, but that's just because you know there's no point in being with someone who doesn't share similar aspirations.

It's not that you don't want to be in love, it's just that you're the least likely sign of the zodiac to be blinded by it. You long to meet someone you can cherish and share your life with, and as you're deeply attractive, wise, funny and refined – you won't have trouble attracting the real thing. But Saturn made you a realist, and he probably taught you quite early on in life to keep your true feelings private until you are quite sure it's safe to reveal them – and this can take time. You may even put off looking for a relationship until you're happy that your career is on the right track, as you're wise enough to consider how much time you would be able to commit to a serious relationship when you're still trying to establish yourself in your chosen field.

When you do meet someone suitable, you don't treat it lightly because you know it could be a lifetime's commitment. Then when you do commit, you're all in – mind, body and soul. When you trust another enough to let your guard down, they'll be delighted to see a side of you that the rest of the word rarely does – loving, gentle, and passionate – with a wickedly deadpan sense of humour.

Working at love

Your Saturn work ethic also applies to relationships. You don't expect even the most wonderful love affairs to be sunshine and rainbows. You understand that nobody is perfect, and you'll include your own flaws and idiosyncrasies in that equation. The best partnerships take effort and, unless you have a predominance of flighty Air or reckless Fire signs in your chart, you will be devoted to making the commitment work. Naturally you'll enjoy setting goals for yourself as a couple – perhaps even working hard to set up a business together.

A traditionalist at heart you'll likely adopt the conventional model for love and romance and apply your high Capricorn standards. You'll choose a stable, albeit rather formal approach with engagement, setting up an impressive home together – and children will be discussed at the appropriate time. Your relationship may appear a little austere to people who don't know you, but your friends and loved ones will see a completely different side. Although always keen to project a grandiose vision of your life together, when it's just you two – you drop the stiff formalities and allow yourself to be playful and vulnerable.

Remember to laugh

The initial exciting stages of romance can be a little overwhelming for your usual cool, calm and collected persona, and you're actually far more comfortable when things settle down. Though this can be a tougher time for your partner, who may feel concerned that you're withdrawing your more spontaneous emotions. This is probably not a conscious decision and is just a sign that you're relaxed enough to be yourself. But you can't expect your partner to be psychic, so try not to let your practical side override or obscure your humorous, affectionate nature. Your ruler Saturn may be something of a 'glass half empty' type of ruling planet, but you could do well to remember that once the hard work is done – you're allowed to enjoy yourself!

Most compatible love signs

Cancer - you share important values with your opposite sign, Cancer. You're both conscientious, cautious and can make heaps of money together.

Scorpio - you're both quite reticent to show how you really feel, but there are fireworks when you do!

Taurus - loyal, steady and determined, you feel safe with Taurus, and these comfort-loving characters will help you to relax and smell the flowers along the way.

Least compatible love signs

Sagittarius - you're quite suspicious of anyone who seems recklessly jolly for no apparent reason.

Aries - they're quite attractive for a while with their big ideas and passions, but they don't have the stamina or vision to back up anything they say.

Gemini - you like tradition, Gemini is faddish, you have serious life goals... they're all chit chat... you don't have time for this!

Work and Career

You are a born business mastermind – the hardest worker in the zodiac – and if you haven't already achieved something prestigious or impressive, you'll be slowly working your way towards it. After all, reaching the top is what goat-people naturally want to do. You size up any challenges in your way with a cool head and learn the skills you need on the steep slope to the top of the mountain.

Born to succeed
As an employee, you're the first person to switch the light on in the office and are often the last to leave. You're trusted with extra heavy workloads because you're known as a steady pair of hands, methodical, conscientious and reliable. You don't quibble, and you'll never tell your boss that something can't be done – you'll find a way even if it means working overtime or learning a whole new set of skills.

Top of the ladder
If you're a Capricorn boss – you're right where you ought to be! Firm but fair, you're a decent boss, who rewards loyalty, and a job well done, but if anyone tries to pull the wool over your eyes you'll not be amused. People need to be honest, put in the hours and, above all, show you the same respect you'd have for a person in your position. Although you're the ultimate professional, when you feel comfortable, your cynical, dry sense of humour comes out to play, surprising anyone who doesn't know you well.

Most compatible colleagues
Gemini - they talk too much, and their silly sense of humour is at odds with your dry wit, but they've got the sparky ideas and creativity that balance out your practical, methodical approach.
Pisces - like you, Pisces prefers to work quietly in the background, and you value their vision and imagination when working on projects together.
Virgo - these practical, organised, conscientious characters are the zodiac's favourite worker bee, and the pair of you are an ambitious, sensible powerhouse.

Least compatible colleagues
Capricorn - two Capricorns together either come to a complete standstill or are ruthlessly competitive.

Leo - Leo needs to be reminded how good they are at everything which, as a self-disciplined Saturnian type, just gets on your goat.
Aquarius - you rarely feel like you're on the same page with Aquarius, but that's because you're not – and neither is anyone else!

Ideal Capricorn Careers
Politician
Accountant
Legal secretary
Estate Agent
Town planner
Mortgage advisor
Lecturer
Entrepreneur
Business analyst
Architect

Well-being
You're blessed with a robust constitution and have the self-discipline to stick to an exercise regime that gets you the results you want. Even the most intimidating fitness challenges don't scare you off, as long as you have the space and time to work incrementally towards mastering your goal. As Capricorn is the sign of the Goat, climbing will be an obvious activity choice, but any form of exercise where you steadily work towards success works best. You have the stamina for long distance running and have the grace and poise to be an elegant ice skater or gymnast.

Food and drink
You have bags of Saturnian self-control when it comes to food and nutrition and find it easier than most to adapt to healthy eating habits. When you're in the zone, you eat regularly, stick to nutritious options, and you don't find it too hard to cut back on calories if you need to. But if you're overworking, food can get forgotten and you'll find yourself relying on 24-hour takeaways or living on caffeine and high energy drinks. This might inject you with the temporary burst of

energy you need to complete your tax return, but eventually you'll feel even more exhausted in the long run.

Don't push yourself

You want to be the best at whatever you are doing, and Saturn can be a hard taskmaster. But beware that you are not pushing yourself too far with exercise, as overdoing it can put pressure on your bones – which can be a weak point. If you're going through a particularly busy or difficult time at work, you might neglect your gym membership or not have time to exercise at all. But getting enough fresh air, natural daylight and feeling connected with the ground, is vital for Earth signs to stay healthy and vibrant. A decent brisk walk every day should keep you ticking over if that's all you have time for.

Sleep is critical and meditation and relaxation methods will help you unwind and focus on something other than work. You, more than anyone else, need to actively make time to be kind to yourself, as you find it easy to self-critical if you feel you're not getting enough done, or feel dissatisfied with your efforts. When you appreciate yourself a little more, you'll find that you're actually one of the few zodiac signs who looks healthier as you age.

AQUARIUS
(21 January – 19 February)

Personality

You are a friendly, inventive, erratic person – the zodiac's non-conformist. The astrological symbol for Aquarius is the Water Carrier, usually depicted as a man pouring water from a large vessel. This connection with water has many thinking Aquarius is a Water sign, but it is not – you're a charismatic, idealistic, Air sign – and you spend more time in your head than any other sign of the zodiac.

The symbol for your ruling planet, future-focussed Uranus, is two wavy lines – which again might look like water, but it actually depicts electricity. You're often described as having an exciting, inventive and volatile personality.

Uranus is the planet of sudden change, connected with rebellion, progression and genius technological breakthroughs. Uranus rules over technology, novelty and ingenuity and in a birth chart its position represents originality, personal freedom, excitement and unexpected surprises.

You're a reformer at heart. You look at humanity's customs, traditions and politics and want to change what's not working to create a brighter vision of society – one that's more tolerant and diverse. Your mission is to raise the planet's consciousness by bringing the world's groups and organisations together for the common good.

Love a mystery

Fascinated by mysteries and esoteric philosophy, subjects such as astrology, ancient religions, conspiracy theories, life in other dimensions or in faraway galaxies, inspire and excite you. If everyone else is getting interested in something, you'll have done it years ago and published a thesis on it. You are tech savvy, quite obsessed with gadgets and the internet. You probably taught yourself how to programme your computer, and you're the first one to know about the latest technological breakthroughs and developments.

Incurable curiosity

Your obsessions also apply to people, which can get you into some awkward situations. If someone finds themselves the object of your curiosity, you'll want to know exactly what makes them tick – right down to the nitty gritty – and you can be quite blunt and sometimes a little shocking in your questions.

You're one of the world's friendliest people, but you can be a little detached from your emotions and this disconnect can cause misunderstandings. Your otherworldly qualities can make you a very glamorous and attractive person, which means that sometimes people you're interested in will get their romantic hopes up. But once you find out everything there is to know about a person, you can become a little disappointed that the mystery wasn't as exciting as you hoped. You might then feel a little embarrassed or explain that you were just being friendly, which could be a bit hurtful for the other party who is no longer the centre of your world. But by then you're gone, lured away by the intense attraction of your new obsession.

Merging with a group or standing alone?

One of your contradictions, and challenging life lessons, is that although you see yourself very much as an independent and unique individual, you love being part of a collective. You feel a sense of family belonging in large groups, whether you're all sports fans, members of a social media group, a political protest organisation or a cosplay fan at a Sci-Fi convention. You long to lose your sense of identity in a group, yet you can be peculiarly lonely.

Follow your own rules

Sometimes you're so ahead of the game that others stop trying to keep up with your avant-garde thinking or accuse you of plucking ideas from thin air. You can appear distant or distracted and, because you don't connect with people on an emotional level, some may think you've lost the plot or are out of touch. But they're mistaken. You're sharp as nails, perhaps even more so when you're concentrating on something really interesting.

Weirdly stubborn

Once you have decided that you're right about something, there is simply no other explanation available. You're extremely clever, and you may even be in touch with a higher intelligence that not everyone else has access to. But regardless of how you reach your decisions, you believe in your own supreme, sometimes irrational, logic. This is another intriguing Aquarian character contradiction, because you're so keen to see change in society, and are completely open-minded about progress. But when it comes to your own personal behaviour, you'll not budge.

Love and relationships

You're the zodiac's humanitarian, everyone's friend, and you're deeply curious about others. If you're on a date with someone interesting, you often flatter them into thinking you're really interested in them because you ask so many questions. They could be forgiven for thinking that they might be rather special. And, of course, you think they're rather wonderful, too, but you're probably just as interested in their mother, or the guy with the weird hat on the other table, or the woman playing the piano in the corner of the restaurant. Not everyone is as attentive or curious as you, without hoping things might progress in a romantic kind of way, and your ardent curiosity can inadvertently lead some hopeful people to think they're in with a chance. This can come as something of a surprise to you, though.

Freedom loving friendliness

You love in a gentle, eternally friendly, way and have an almost scientific interest in the people around you. But you're a bit out of your depth when it comes to physical feelings such as lust, jealousy or passion. As a lofty Air sign, you live in your big eccentric, colourful mind, and go where your eternal curiosity leads you. You're a free spirit, and often when you've discovered everything about the person you're scrutinizing, your attention is grabbed by someone, or something else. Uranus has you firmly focused on the future, so you can hop from an obsession with one person to the next, without much trouble.

Different kinds of love

You're delightfully cool and glamorous, and exude an air of mystery, which means you're not short of admirers. But for you to get really hooked on someone they'll probably have an intriguing, rather aloof, air. When you do meet someone who has you entranced, you may be as giddy as a teenager in the first flush of romance, walking along the street bumping into lamp posts. You'll be excited and a little disturbed that you've found someone who is different to everyone else. Though it won't be long before you start analysing what it all really means.

You're a supremely logical creature, and love can be a tricky concept for you to get your head around. You think love is just love, caring for humanity as group, looking out for each other as a collective. When one person means everything to you, you'll be perplexed but excited, after all it's a new experience. But you'll wonder what is expected of you in return.

Contrary and independent

You're an oddball, Aquarius, you love the weirdest ideas and freely travel the globe pursuing them – and genuinely don't expect other people to move to a Japanese commune, believe in aliens, or come to live with you in your converted ambulance. But you're not about to give up any of your strange beliefs or peculiar lifestyle to settle down in a semi-detached house and have a family. That's far too predictable for you, unless you find a workable compromise. Your partner knew what you were like before you committed yourself to one another. If they've stuck with you through your stint as a waterslide tester or an international trampolinist, they'll probably already love this about you, and won't expect you to attend church every Sunday, or sit on the couch every night... though you may well decide to try either of these for a while, just to prove them wrong!

Emotional conundrum

You're often embarrassed by emotions – your own and others' – and you'll do your best to keep your own hidden. You tend to dissociate from unpleasant feelings like jealousy, anger, aggression or neediness. But when your logical mind accepts that having to deal with *all* emotions – the dark ones and the beautiful ones – is what makes us human, you'll find there's a nobleness in reasoning that you're only human too.

Most compatible love signs

Libra - gentle, harmonious, romantic Libra can teach you how to love without throwing any awkward emotional tantrums.
Leo - you're in awe of Leo's willingness to please others and secretly think they know something you don't.

Aquarius - you're unique and they're unique. You both don't mind sleeping on futons, plan to build a dwelling out of old car doors, and breed iguanas.

Least compatible love signs

Taurus - Taurus like to know what they're having for dinner tonight, but the last time you ate a regular meal you were in prison!

Scorpio - you're very curious about Scorpio because you know they're hiding something but are afraid to find out exactly what it is.

Cancer - you can't always tell what you did to upset Cancer, but you know it must have been really bad.

Work and career

It may take you a while before you find a career that will keep you interested. You'll happily investigate, experiment and explore while you're young, finding a position that doesn't make you want to staple your fingers to a desk out of boredom. You'll have no trouble being offered work because although your unconventional approach may put some people off initially, they soon discover that you're an eccentric little goldmine.

Unconventional genius

You have something of an absent-minded professor reputation at work. You come up with genius money-making ideas while you're on your tea break but have half an eye on the cricket score in important meetings. It's not that you don't follow rules to be difficult, it's just that your mind is doing something far more interesting than remembering when to eat lunch. You already know how to run cars on water, teleport to different planets and cure the common cold – but you got so caught up in your next thought that you forgot to tell anyone about it.

Revolutionary spirit

You want to make society a better place and you're not afraid to think outside of the box - though some of it is so ahead of time it needs to go back into the box until the rest of the world is ready! You have a radar for what people are about to do and how to improve people's lives with your original solutions. You're not that interested in rank and hierarchy in your job, and you genuinely don't care what other people think of you. It's never all about the money or the status for Aquarius; it's about ripping up old traditions and customs that are no longer working and replacing them with brilliant new ideas that will revolutionize the planet.

Most compatible colleagues
Libra - you need Libra's diplomacy and understanding of social conventions, as these are something of an alien concept to you.
Gemini - a brilliant mind who likes working on a team – perfect! Just don't expect them to be the same person tomorrow.
Sagittarius - you both have insatiable curiosity and big ideas – together you change the world for the better.

Least compatible colleagues
Aquarius - what planet is this person on? Oh, damn – it's your planet!
Aries - these guys can be bossy, while you generally wait for a consensus. They can also be bad tempered, which is not your bag at all.
Capricorn - they're clever, but a bit too conventional to appreciate your genius… and a bit too cynical.

Ideal Aquarius careers
Scientist
Politician
Professor
Computer programmer
Engineer
Air traffic controller
Astrologer
Social enterprise professional
Alternative therapist
Inventor

Well-being

As a mentally focussed Air sign, sometimes you get so caught up in what you're doing that you're genuinely surprised that your body exists at all, never mind that it's complaining it's hungry, or stiff from sitting in the same position. It can be hard for you to get really motivated about moving your body because it can take you away from what you're really interested in.

Long nights staring at your computer or using all your energy trying to solve a scientific puzzle, could leave you feeling frazzled. Sometimes your body appears to just switch itself off for a quick reset... more commonly known to the other zodiac signs as 'sleep'.

Exercise isn't something you like to schedule or think of as routine. You get bored with any repetitive physical movement – and going to the gym at the same time every day won't appeal much. But as an extroverted, social sign of the zodiac, being around others lifts your spirits and fills you with energy, so team sports and busy classes will prove more fulfilling. A bit of a tech nut, you'll be able to source virtual classes or activities too.

Food and drink

You may have studied nutrition very closely and have a better understanding than most about which vitamins and minerals you really need – and which to avoid. You may have a very progressive attitude to food, eating a pure diet that focuses only on what your body requires, perhaps as a vegan or through practising strict calorie control. Green smoothies after fasting, unpronounceable vegetables from exotic countries for lunch, and a nut-based protein bar designed for astronauts if you feel peckish later. You're an unpredictable eater, and anything too samey drives you crazy after a while. This might result in some unusual fads, such as existing on caffeine until 3pm, then consuming only red food for two hours with raw liver before bed.

Alternative treatments

Naturally rebellious, it's not just food norms you'll question. You'll quibble the knowledge and advice offered by most traditional healthcare givers. Besides, haven't they even heard of emotional freedom technique, past life regression, or reflexology for your headache? You'll do your own research obsessively, and if there's an outlandish theory that fits your current zany idea, you'll try it. Weirdly, the stranger a treatment sounds to you, the more likely it will be to work for you.

PISCES (19 February – 20 March)

Personality

You are Pisces, the Fish, the most compassionate and spiritual of all the zodiac signs, and your empathy is almost telepathic. Your zodiac symbol is depicted as two fish swimming in opposite directions, representing your constant flipping between fantasy and reality, and your immensely sensitive nature and boundless imagination means it's sometimes challenging for you to feel rooted in the here and now. You're a deeply intuitive and emotional Water sign, reflecting the fathomless, mysterious power of the ocean, and sometimes you feel swept away on waves of feeling. You are ruled by elusive, ethereal Neptune, the planet of magic and illusion, and you have a reputation for being the most wonderfully creative person, even if you sometimes view the world through rose-tinted spectacles.

Each sign of the zodiac is thought to embody a little of the wisdom and lessons of the signs preceding it. As Pisces is the last of the 12 signs, you have absorbed all the wisdom, joy, pain and fears of the other zodiac characters. This explains why you have a rather blurred, obscure sense of self, and why you are more tuned to the collective psyche than anyone else.

Startlingly intuitive

It's your job to find beauty and meaning in the real, bricks-and-mortar, warts and all, everyday world. For you to feel truly alive and happy, your lesson is to step outside your limitless imagination and learn to be a person in your own right. As someone who understands the suffering of life on earth more intensely than most, you can form the deepest connections with the people who need your faith, kindness and compassion.

Powerhouse of talent

The flipside to being aware of life's joys as well as disappointments is that you know real beauty when you find it. A pretty weed growing through a crack in the pavement can fill your heart with joy, and a smile from a stranger in a supermarket instantly restores your faith in humanity. Your intense sensitivity allows creativity to stream through you, and you're never happier than when in full flow. You have too little ego, and value your privacy too much to thrust your ideas and creations on the outside world, and you usually underestimate your capabilities. But creatively you're capable of creating the most moving pieces of music, evocative poetry, and exquisite works of art.

Escapist dreamworlds

On some level you can't quite believe you have incarnated into this clunky, ugly world where everyone feels lonely. When you're tuned into other planes of existence, earthly life can feel heavy. Your desire for escapism is probably the most difficult for you to master because why go through the effort and disappointment of finding a job, looking for someone to love, and taking care of yourself, when you can get lost in books, sex or daydreaming? And, of course, there's alternative realities to visit where you can blot out the real world completely.

The meaning of money

You either see money as the root of all evil, or as an elusive resource that pours through you like water through a sieve. You can't say no to people in trouble just as you can't ignore those heart-breaking television campaigns for animal charities or for people who desperately need help. You'll see one sad looking doggy and give your last ten pounds to an animal shelter before realising you need it for your rent, bus fare to work – or your dinner!

You are best suited to work where you are able to relieve others' pain or disillusionment, maybe in a job campaigning for a homeless charity, as a doctor or nurse, a psychotherapist or as an alternative health practitioner.

You'll also attract money by exchanging it for the wonderful manifestations of your rich imagination. But as you're inclined to underestimate your talents, you might need a little encouragement to get started. If you haven't already, you could begin by building an online audience for your astonishing art, fine dressmaking skills, or marvellously inventive fiction.

Don't give yourself away

Not everyone is as open and understanding as you. You're a wonderful listener, and your empathic nature encourages others to share their secrets, worries and woes. And as you have an impressionable, boundary-less Neptune as your ruling planet, it's hard for you to separate your own thoughts and feelings from those of others. This is why it's important that you get enough time on your own to recover your sense of self. You have unparalleled skills for bringing beauty and happiness to others through your selfless deeds – and just being yourself. But before you give yourself away, you must work on what it is that you love doing and what makes you happy. If you're going to inspire, uplift and encourage people who are confused about where they're going – you can't also be lost!

Love and relationships

Pisces is depicted as two fish swimming in opposite directions, simultaneously experiencing conscious and unconscious, heaven and hell, and nowhere do these extremes feel more apparent than in your love life. As far as you're concerned, the perfect union of romantic love is the closest to heaven you can be. You know that the merging of twin souls could make you feel whole again, perhaps because you've already had a taste of it in this life – or been there in a past one. Unconsciously or not, you wish for romantic love to save you, to swallow you whole and tell you that nothing else matters.

The poet of the zodiac

You are eternally hopeful that you'll meet the perfect person who makes all the pain go away and gives you meaning to your life. But sometimes in your love dreams you project what you so badly want onto another person, and you'll make-believe it's true. You may have already thought you were in love a few times only to have stark reality pull you aside for a few harsh words.

You want to believe the lovely things you hear other people say are true, and learning that people are 'just being nice' to avoid hurting your feelings is a bitter pill to swallow. You hurt like nobody else, but because you allow yourself to feel so much emotion, you are rather brilliant at processing your feelings and moving on.

You're quite hypnotised by the lure of losing yourself in another, and the possibility of romance is so enticing that you can swim from one affair to the other, in search of the person who completely sweeps you away. And sometimes you do meet someone who fits the bill… for a while. But when they eventually reveal themselves to be real people with morning breath and terrible taste in music, you feel a little cheated.

Fairy tale fantasy

You're so in love with love that you can't help but hope the next person you feel attracted to will prove all the fairy tales right. But that's a tall order for anyone to live up to. Your intended may even feel that you're looking right through them to some mystical reflection that bears little resemblance to her or him. If you're being realistic you might even feel, in some of your less limerent moments, that perhaps your reverence has very little to do with the flesh and blood person who just cooked you scrambled eggs or bought you tickets to see your favourite film.

Truth in relationships

When you care for others as deeply as you do it's essential that you try to see things clearly, and that's not that easy with ambiguous, hazy Neptune as your ruling planet. When you want something to be true, you'll often take the line of least resistance by pulling the wool over your own eyes rather than dealing with what's really there. You find confrontation hugely uncomfortable and will avoid asking loved ones direct questions for fear of finding out the truth. But that's exactly what you need to keep yourself rooted in the real world.

Honesty is what you need most from your relationships because when you become more skilled at dealing with your own reality, you'll be a much better judge of other people's character and intentions – which should cut a heap of heartbreak from your life.

Beautiful tragedies

You have an amazing ability to find beauty and magic in sadness and tragedy – and you can be strangely attracted to people who face real difficulties. But you'll need to have your reality head screwed on if you feel the line between compassion and romantic love beginning to get fuzzy. Go in with your eyes fully open and enlist some practical Earth sign friends to keep your heart from slipping into fantasy mode.

Most compatible love signs

Scorpio - you're one of the few people that can see past Scorpio's deadpan expression to the deep well of emotion inside – and you like it!
Virgo - your opposite sign of Virgo gently and kindly shows you how to live in the real world without making it seem too unpleasant.
Cancer - you're on the same level emotionally, both sensitive and careful with each other's hearts.

Least compatible love signs

Aries - there's no sugar coating with Aries; they're as blunt and on-the-nose as they come. You need a bit more fairy tale and stardust than that!
Gemini - Gemini usually floats on the surface of things when you like to dive in as deeply as possible.

Leo - you need time away from people to feel like an individual, and Leo feeds off attention to feel like they're valid.

Work and Career

You absorb the atmosphere of the pond you swim in, so your working environment is particularly important to you. In your younger years you may spend a few years swimming from place to place, discovering what appeals and your preferred way of working. You prefer working quietly in the background, anyone who thinks you're not doing anything of note is usually deceived. When it's your time to talk about what you've been working on, or your employer asks for results, you'll modestly render everyone speechless with your imaginative, well thought-out piece of creative genius.

Artistic and imaginative

You're the artist of the zodiac, able to communicate what cannot be otherwise expressed, through paint, music, pottery, writing or fashion design. Your ability to take on your surroundings also means that you're a brilliant actor and mimic, so when you make a character study, you become the person you are focusing on.

Swim to the top

You're an even-tempered, slightly reclusive boss and responsibility can sit uneasily on your shoulders. Unless you have a smattering of workaholic Capricorn or Virgo in your chart – people come first. If someone on your team is sick or has to lend a hand in a family drama, you'll usher them out the door yourself, with instructions for bedrest or sincere wishes for their cat's welfare. And you live by the same rules. If someone needs you, they're your priority.

Most compatible colleagues

Aquarius - these guys love working with your brilliant imagination and they can add an ingenious, inventive touch that makes your ideas sing.
Capricorn - you work well with these quiet, hardworking types, and they respect your need to be left to your own devices.

Gemini - you both live in your heads, and you can take any Gemini idea and visualise it into something spectacular – and they never run out of inspiring thoughts.

Least compatible colleagues

Sagittarius - you'll have to make a big noise to grab the attention of Sagittarius, so you'd rather they just left you in peace to get on with looking after the future of humanity.

Libra - they can't make up their mind and you can be disorganised... It's a distracting mix that rarely comes up with a solid plan.

Cancer - you're both good friends, but at work the pair of you are so woolly together that neither of you are completely sure what the other is meant to be doing.

Ideal Pisces careers

Artist
Charity fundraiser
Chemist
Actor
Dancer
Nurse
Psychologist
Priest
Swimmer
Chiropodist

Well-being

Graceful, delicate and a little shy, as an emotional Water sign, you usually exist inside your emotions and your imagination. Ruled by magical but confusing Neptune, you may start off with good intentions about losing weight or exercising, but you become disillusioned when you don't see fast results or start to feel uncomfortable.

Your imagination can be the most active thing about you, and because you're such a visual person, creating a mood board with images of people or clothes you like the look of, will help you keep on track. You might feel too self-conscious exercising in a group environment, or mortified by a personal trainer's close scrutiny, so going it alone at home or joining an internet class – with your camera off – should keep things more private.

Dancing is a much-loved Pisces activity, as it's linked with the feet – the Piscean area of the body. Like a fish shimmying through water, you're an elegant, gliding mover. And, of course, you're literally right in your element swimming and being in the water and going for a quick dip in the ocean can feel like a religious experience.

Food and drink

If you're feeling stressed or anxious you can absent-mindedly use food as a way to stop you from focusing on what is really bothering you. You might even binge eat – and drink – to level out your changeable moods. And as far as you're concerned, it doesn't matter if the glass is half-full or half-empty, there's still plenty of room for wine!

Your first instincts when not feeling great are usually Neptunian – and therefore escapist in nature. Turning to alcohol, chocolate or any mood-altering substance might work for a while, but unfortunately most of the addictive things in life aren't very good for you. Luckily there are other, more satisfying, ways to escape… meditation, sex, even losing yourself in an amazing book, or singing in a choir will all help you rise above your mundane existence for long enough to make you feel part of something more beautiful again.

Wholesome approach

Another way to make sure you're firmly rooted in the here and now is to treat emotional issues as seriously as you do physical ones. Seeking counselling or emotional therapy will make you much more aware of any escapist tendencies and will help you stay grounded and present.